The
Navy of the Republic of Texas

1835-1845

=By=
Dr. Alex Dienst
Temple, Texas
1909

Notice

In many older books, foxing (or discoloration) occurs and, in some instances, print lightens with wear and age. Reprinted books, such as this, often duplicate these flaws, notwithstanding efforts to reduce or eliminate them. The pages of this reprint have been digitally enhanced and, where possible, the flaws eliminated in order to provide clarity of content and a pleasant reading experience.

The Navy of the Republic of Texas 1835-1845

Originally published:
Temple, Texas
1909

Reprinted:
Janaway Publishing, Inc.
2011

Janaway Publishing, Inc.
732 Kelsey Ct.
Santa Maria, California 93454
(805) 925-1038
www.janawaygenealogy.com

ISBN: 978-1-59641-240-8

Made in the United States of America

Preface

The citizen of Texas, traveling in the United States, is often-times shocked to find that comparatively few people are aware that Texas for ten years was an independent Republic. However, this ignorance is by no means confined to people outside of Texas; even informed Texans are surprised to learn that Texas in her struggle for independence, and the maintaining of that independence, possessed a Navy, powerful enough to aid her in the struggle, and to successfully combat every effort of Mexico to regain her territory.

While in comparison with the great navies of to-day, the navy of the infant Republic was exceedingly small, yet it was greater in its infancy, and better organized, than was the navy of the United States in 1776, and the first year of that memorable struggle for independence. The part that the Texas Navy acted from 1835 to 1846 has never been related. The leading historians of Texas repeatedly testify that the navy was a valuable factor in securing Texas independence, but while admitting this much, they almost without exception fail to chronicle any events in which the navy participated; nothing is said regarding its organization, maintenance, or successes, and the few historians that do give it notice have allowed numerous errors to creep into their statements, and succeeding historians have repeated the errors.

While students may differ in opinion as to what would have ultimately been the fate of the country we now call Texas, none will dispute the assertion that Texas could not at the time have won her independence and maintaind it as she did, without the navy. This is an incontrovertible fact that I shall repeatedly prove in this history. Without a navy to protect her extensive coast, transports laden with thousands of Mexican soldiers, and thousands of tons of provisions, could have been landed in Texas at all times by Mexico, and would have been landed; and this overwhelming force would have conquered the Texans. Furthermore, Texas could have been certain of no supplies from New Orleans, whence came three-fourths of all her troops, supplies, and cash, if the carrying vessels in the trade between New Orleans and Texas had not been reasonably sure of protection against Mexican war vessels. Few merchants in New Orleans would have been willing to hazard their precious cargoes, with the probability of a Mexican war vessel capturing the same, which happened at times even *with* a Texas

Navy, and *without* such a Navy, would have been the rule. Another great benefit of the navy to the struggling revolutionists was the revenue derived from its prizes and captures, and by the Government acknowledged as an invaluable contribution in time of need. Another way in which it was a help was the able way in which it blocked the enemy's ports, and harassed the commerce of Mexico, and by this means proving to the United States, and leading foreign governments, the stability of the young Republic, and her ability to keep the independence she had won at San Jacinto. The ability thus demonstrated to the world won her recognition as an independent Republic by foreign powers.

My attention was attracted to this field of labor many years ago, by the numerous references I found to the Texas Navy in the files of New Orleans newspapers of 1835-45. As early as 1897 I was concentrating my efforts in securing Texas historical material bearing upon the navy. In October, 1900, in an article on the value of the New Orleans newspaper files of the Texas Revolutionary period, which appeared in the Quarterly of the Texas State Historical Association, I made the statement that I would write a history of the navy of the Revolution. Upon further reflection I concluded to write the history of the navy throughout its existence, and this, necessitating much more research and labor, has occupied all my spare moments for the past few years. Had I written this preface before I finished the work, I should no doubt have remarked that it was a "labor of love"—writing the preface at the close of nine years of unremitting labor, irksome, tedious, with the drudgery of copying, correcting, and so forth, the expression would be anything but truthful; only those who have labored similarly can appreciate fully what toil and self-denial are required to gather, classify, record, reflect upon, and select the material for such a work as this. I would not have attempted to carry out the work if I had thought anyone else would perform it; but having much valuable material bearing upon the subject, and my inclination leaning that way, I was compelled by the responsibility I felt to write what I have, in order that this much of the history of our beloved Texas should not be lost.

As to my qualifications for the work I have here undertaken, I have none to boast of, save a deep love for the perpetuation of the daring and heroic deeds of the first American pioneers of Texas. Not a native Texan, though coming here before I was twenty-one, and not related to any character in this history, and not having been acquainted with a single survivor, and only in one instance being acquainted with the descendant of such, the writer of this book has an advantage that a contemporaneous historian can not possess. I have been free from prejudice, and not biased by friendship or ties of blood to view any act, save on the principles of truth. In the course of the history, necessarily, conflicting evidences from most reliable sources at times occur; in such cases I have given the gentlemen on both sides the credit of being sincere in their statements—unless unquestionable proof shows the contrary; it has been my aim to present controversial matter from the viewpoint of each individual, and let the reader form his own conclusions, if there is any doubt. Where the original documents have been accessible, and the proof is clearly for one man or another, I have never hesitated to declare, "Thou art the man," and having the opportunity to read all the documents in full—whereas many are here only alluded to, or quoted in part—I have been better qualified to do this than my predecessors, who have here and there had a fragment or a sketch to guide them, and have written more to defend or advance an opinion than to review the history impartially and give the absolute facts. There would have been certain advantages in writing a history of the navy fifty years ago; but it is confidently believed by the author that the advantages of collecting all materials at this late day, and sifting them, and winnowing the good from the bad, will outweigh the disadvantages that time brings in the destruction of historical materials.

As regards the collecting of material for this history, the author believes it will be worthy of a short space. While I have been peculiarly fortunate in my search, and have unearthed some material that would have been inaccessible to anyone else, there is no excuse for historians having neglected to mention the navy for lack of material; much of value could have at all times been found at Austin by a little research; it is true that a great deal of matter relative to naval history was burned at Austin in 1855, and in other fires, but still, the various departments had documents supplemental and explanatory of the navy. According to the testimony of Judge C. W. Raines, in his "Bibliography of Texas," the departments have never been so well investigated by historians as the rich material there would justify. As the material accessible to the historian stamps the value of the work in a large measure, I desire to give a brief description of some of the material used in the work. The history is in two parts. Texas had two distinct navies; and part one recites the history of the first naval establishment from 1835 to 1839. Part two describes the second naval establishment from 1839 to 1846.

In the history of the first navy, I get much of my material from the New Orleans newspaper files—of which I have the only known collection from 1835 to 1837. All official documents such as acts, decrees, etc., of the Texas Government were sent to William Bryan, Texas agent, in New Orleans, and also to William Christy, a true friend of Texas; their collections, made during the revolution and carefully preserved by them, came into my possession some ten years ago. Many of these documents have no duplicates, and are now for the first time cited in a history of Texas. The late Judge C. W. Raines, in 1898, drew my attention to the papers of William A. Tennison of the Texas Navy. I purchased these, and found them very reliable and valuable. Judge J. G. Tod, while Secretary of State, furnished me with copies of all documents relative to the Texas Navy, in the Department of State: in the work itself I have taken pleasure in giving testimony to his good will. One of the most helpful works, and an indispensable one to the worker in Texas history, not residing in Austin, is the Gammel *"Reprint of Texas Laws."* Through the kindness of Secretary Long, of the U. S. N. Department, I was furnished by the Librarian of Naval War Records, copies of valuable documents, and have had forwarded to me some rare books, from which I made accurate copies of pamphlets they contained, bearing upon the quarrel between Commodore E. W. Moore and President Sam Houston upon the incorporation of Texas Naval Officers into the U. S. Navy. Moore's *Appeal* is probably the most valuable single work relative to the second navy of Texas; but one copy of this is existing at this late day, so far as I know, and I have found it absolutely reliable as regards documents cited, being, as it is, a work especially to vindicate one character and attacking another, the views and conclusions reached by the author must be carefully examined before being accepted. The early newspapers of Texas, 1835-45, have been very helpful, and many valuable facts gathered from them. The earlier historians of Texas, Edward, Newell, Foote, and Kennedy, wrote their histories before 1841, and of course did not have the opportunity given them to say much concerning this arm of the national defense; those who came after them should have given the navy a more prominent place. Yoakum, who had very excellent opportunities, gives about seven pages to the navy; his statements contain several errors. Thrall, including biographical sketches, gives about four pages, containing some good matter, but also a number of errors. Bancroft gives the same space as Yoakum, with very little new material. Brown, who had splendid opportunities for getting accurate information, makes gross errors in the four pages he devotes to the Navy. Morphis has some four pages, copied from the other histories; he presents no new matter. Pennybacker's school history, used in all public schools, is of course intended only as a primary work, and not much original research work is expected in such a work; yet, it appears to me that more space might be devoted to the navy which did so much for Texas than appears in this volume; less than one page is devoted to the first navy, and not one word is said in regard to Commodore Moore and the second Navy; while four times as much space is given to an alleged speech of Travis, which is the first time mentioned in the *Texas Almanac* nearly forty years after it was supposed to have been delivered, and only vouched for by a man named Rose, who was too cowardly to remain in the Alamo.

In writing the history of the Texas Navy my aim has been to write in such a manner as to entertain the critical student, and the general reader. I am desirous of avoiding a parade of honesty in acknowledging the sources of facts given in this history, but there has been such a shameful method of appropriating other men's researches, without due acknowledgment by historians, that I have become peculiarly sensitive to withholding credit where it is due. To the critical student these acknowledgments enhance the value of the work; to the general reader I can only express the hope that he will let the notes interrupt as little as possible the flow of thought, and that they might not unduly detract or mar the interest which the facts related are calculated to awaken. The laws of unity must also be violated in a work of this nature; certain facts and incidents pertaining to the navy, although not necessarily belonging to any particular chapter, must be mentioned somewhere; to weave them gracefully into the narrative is out of the question, at times, so the best that was possible was done. In gathering material for this history, I have always gone to the sources where accessible; and given credit where it is due. In crediting an article, I have given the preference of authority to the earliest and most reliable official acts, such as: Official Proclamations, Acts, Decrees, Ordinances, Convention and Council and Legislative doings; after these, log books, official letters, newspapers and pamphlets, journals of officers, histories and miscellaneous matter, such as unofficial letters and reminiscences. In the standard histories, such as Kennedy, Yoakum, Brown and Bancroft, credit or reference to the source is not always given by them. Bancroft is better than the rest in this respect; but in no case is material taken from these sources, if the credit is due elsewhere: in other words, if a reliable newspaper article gives information in 1836 that is exactly the same as embodied in one of the above histories, and the history does not give credit, I give credit to the newspaper that first furnished the article, and so, if Yoakum and Bancroft both mention the same fact, I give Yoakum credit and not Bancroft, as Yoakum wrote some forty-five years before Bancroft. And so, too, respecting official documents: wherever possible, the original documents are cited, rather than excerpts made from them, and incorporated in some history. At all times the sources have been most diligently worked for, and where documents are rare, attention is called to their existence and their location at this day. The author is unwilling to send forth this book without specially mentioning a few friends, who, by their encouraging words and efforts, have cheered him on when his zeal was flagging. Mention has already been made of the kindness of the late Judge Raines and Judge Tod. In the body of the work I allude to favors shown be by the late Dr. George P. Garrison of the State University. The late Lester Bugbee inspired me with a desire to do something towards unfolding and developing Texas History; and William Winkler has put me under obligations for kindnesses; and I desire to thank Eugene C. Barker of the State University for helpful suggestions.

ALEX. DIENST.

Temple, Texas, Jan. 1, 1909.

Table of Contents

		Page
Chapter I.	The "Correo Mexicano" & "San Felipe"	1
Chapter II.	Organization of the Navy	9
Chapter III.	The Texan Privateers	20
Chapter IV.	Naval Vessels Bought and Equipped	32
Chapter V.	The "Liberty"	39
Chapter VI.	Texan Man of War "Invincible"	42
Chapter VII.	Texan Man of War "Brutus"	51
Chapter VIII.	Texan Man of War "Independence"	55
Chapter IX.	Measures taken to procure another Navy	66
Chapter X.	Early Troubles of the New Navy	77
Chapter XI.	Cruise of the Texan Navy 1840-1841	82
Chapter XII.	Texas and Yucatan Alliance	94
Chapter XIII.	The Mutiny on Board the "San Antonio"	107
Chapter XIV.	Moore's Efforts to Fit Out the Fleet at New Orleans and His Agreement With Yucatan	111
Chapter XV.	Engagements of Texan and Mexican Navies off the Yucatan Coast and Houston's Proclamation Against Moore	128
Chapter XVI.	Dismissal of Moore, Lothrop, and Snow From Service and Trial of Moore	135
Chapter XVII.	Final Disposition of the Vessels of the Navy	140

To My Booke

"My Little Pinnance, strike thy sailes,
Let slip thy anchor; the winde failes,
And seamen oft in calmes do feare
That foule and boistrous weather's neare;
If a robustious storme should rise,
And bluster from censorious eyes,
Al though the swelling waves be rough,
And proud, thy harbour's safe enough.
Rest, rest awhile, till ebbing tides
 Shall make thee stanche and breme thy sides,
When windes shall serve, hoist up thy saile,
And fly before a prosp'rous gale;
That all the Coasters may resort,
And bid thee welcome to thy port."

Dr. Alex Dienst

Appreciation

Dr. Alex Dienst was born in St. Louis, Missouri, in 1870, and moved to Texas at the age of twenty-one. After studying medicine and dentistry in Philadelphia, he established himself as a dentist in Temple, Texas, and practiced his profession intermittently until his death in 1938. He became an enthusiastic student of Texas history and a collector of books and source materials dealing particularly with the Texas revolution, which he generously placed at the disposal of historical scholars. As his collection grew, he found that it tended to emphasize the history of the Texas Navy, about which historians had written very little, and he determined to put in its proper light the important service of the navy in the establishment of the Republic of Texas. His study appeared in four numbers of *The Quarterly* of the Texas State Historical Association, beginning with the issue of January, 1909. This copy, with a slight rearrangement of the original make-up, is one that he re-printed privately for distribution to friends. It is comprehensive and soundly based on a complete understanding of source material, and will always be a useful and authoritative study of the subject.

For twenty years Dr. Dienst was a valuable member of the Executive Council and for three years was President of the Texas State Historical Association. He was keenly interested in politics and people, and one of the intermissions from his professional office was employed as postmaster of Temple by appointment of President Woodrow Wilson. Time saw greater and great absorption in his study of Texas history. Besides his history of the Navy, he published in *The Southwestern Historical Quarterly,* in 1917, a significant collection of "Contemporary Poetry of the Texas Revolution," compiled mostly from Texas and New Orleans newspapers. During his later years he gave much time to the promotion of his beloved specialty in free public lectures on what he called "the grand theme of the Pioneers of Texas." To sponsors of these lectures and patriotic societies he made three stipulations: (1) that his bare traveling expenses be reimbursed; (2) that no admission be charged; and (3) that he be allowed to finish his speech, which he warned, "means two hours and fifteen minutes speaking by a very great lover of Texas history."

Dr. Dienst was a genial, kindly man, critical but tolerant, and with a lively sense of humor which he could apply to himself. Much of his great collection of Texana is now appropriately a part of the library of The University of Texas.

>EUGENE C. BARKER,
>Professor of American History,
>The University of Texas.

THE NAVY OF THE REPUBLIC OF TEXAS.

THE FIRST NAVY OF TEXAS.

I. THE CORREO MEXICANO AND THE SAN FELIPE.

Throughout the first half of 1835 serious misunderstandings and difficulties had occurred between the merchants and the collector of the maritime customhouse of Galveston, Texas, in relation to the collection of duties.[1] In the hope of averting trouble and of bringing about a peaceable adjustment, the *ayuntamiento* of Liberty, in the deparment of Nacogdoches, issued a manifesto[2] to the effect "that the revenue laws, like all other political laws, are to be respected by all those who come within the legitimate sphere of their actions; and although these laws may be unwise, to resist them by force is more unwise and ill timed than the laws themselves." The manifesto goes on to say that the duties are oppressive, disproportionate, and in need of modification; but that this change must be a legal one, and not brought about by force. And the dissatisfied citizens are urged to abstain from any violent measures towards the collector of the maritime customs of Galveston. Notwithstanding this conservative counsel, Captain Tenorio and his small garrison stationed at Anahuac to guard the port against smuggling and afford protection to the collector of customs, were attacked by William B. Travis and fifty armed Texans and forced to leave. This act of the Texans and Americans at Anahuac was condemned by the municipality of Liberty

---

[1] The author must refer the general reader who is desirous of becoming acquainted with the details leading up to the revolution in Texas, to the histories of the State, and to such monographic accounts as relate to this period. Only such matter of a general nature will be inserted as is necessary to introduce and present a connected account of the movements of the naval vessels of Texas and Mexico.

[2] *Texas Republican*, May 30, 1835. The manifesto is dated April 7, 1835; Edward (*History of Texas*, 235-38) erroneously prints it under the date of June 1. See Eugene C. Barker, *Difficulties of a Mexican Revenue Officer*, in THE QUARTERLY, IV, 194, note 3.

"The alcalde in his separate capacity combined the larger powers of our mayors and justices of the peace. The duties of the regidores assimilated

and the Central Committee.[1] A sensational account of the attack on the revenue officer was carried to General Cos, who, being not yet aware that it did not carry with it the endorsement of the majority of the Texans, in July ordered the sloop of war *Correo Mexicano*, commanded by Captain T. M. Thompson, to the scene of action to protect Mexican commerce.[2] In violation of orders,[3] Thompson bullied the citizens and traders at Anahuac, threatened to burn the town,[4] and proved himself utterly unfit for the delicate task of upholding Mexican authority and calming the excitement of the people.

Thompson's most serious mistake was the capture of the American brig *Tremont*. This vessel was in the Texan trade,[5] and though I have searched diligently I can find nowhere any reason given for his attack.[6] No historian gives even a hint as to his

to those of our alderman, and the sindicos corresponded with recorders. These sitting together composed the Ayuntamiento, which had jurisdiction over the entire community."—Lynch, *The Bench and Bar of Texas*, 20.

[1]Edward, *History of Texas*, 235; Kennedy, *Texas*, II, 92-94; Yoakum, *History of Texas*, I, 339; Bancroft, *North Mexican States and Texas*, II, 156. (These works will be henceforth cited in this narrative respectively as Edward, Kennedy, Yoakum, and Bancroft.) But Edward errs in citing here as proof of censure for an act which occurred June 30 a proclamation which he dates June 1, and which was actually issued April 17 and published May 30. See above, p. 1, note 2.

[2]Captain Thompson was an Englishman by birth, and was at this time an adopted citizen of Mexico. He had been in the Mexican service some years. His appearance was unprepossessing, and he was reported to be striving to make a fortune by fair means or foul. He was misunderstood at this time, or his character changed materially; for later on he was very kind to Texas prisoners, and ultimately took the side of the Texans. Edward, 248; Yoakum, I, 356; Bancroft, II, 161. Edward (248) and Kennedy (II, 94) claim that his instructions were to make observations, and find out whether the collector and his men had been massacred by the Americans, as had been reported, and return to Matamoras as soon as possible with his information.

[3]Colonel Ugartechea himself admitted this much in a letter to Stephen F. Austin, dated October 4, 1835, saying, "I know you are right to complain of Thompson's proceedings, which I still less approve, as they were arbitrary; he having no authority to act in such manner." Yoakum, I, 356. Captain Thompson issued a "Proclamation to the citizens of Anahuac," July 26, 1835. It is printed in full in Brown, *Life of Henry Smith*, 63, *et seq.*

[4]Travis to Bowie, July 30, 1835, MS.

[5]Pennybacker, *History of Texas*, 117, calls the *Tremont* a United States naval vessel. This is a mistake; it was a trading vessel.

[6]The explanation apparently is that Thompson had arbitrarily declared

reason. The nearest explanation I can find in his favor is derived from an article in the New Orleans newspapers, signed "Seventy-six." It is a reply to a defence of Thompson which I am unfortunately unable to locate, but from the communication of "Seventy-six" it can be gathered that Thompson's defender asserted that he was sent to the Texas coast to interrupt the importation of negroes from Cuba. I will give the comment in part, as it will also furnish some details of the capture which I can find nowhere else:

Mr. Editor: My attention was last evening called to an article in an evening journal, headed "Texas and the United States District Attorney at New Orleans, vs. Louisiana, Mississippi, Alabama and Arkansas," which contains a most violent and abusive attack against the individuals in this country whose feelings have been aroused in favor of an oppressed and deceived people, strugling to maintain their rights of civil liberty: an attempt to assert the innocence of Captain Thompson now waiting a trial for piracy. They are also charged with bringing negroes into Texas, in violation of the constitution of 1824, while in fact there is no provision in the constitution prohibiting the introduction of negroes from Cuba or elsewhere. The writer adds that Captain Thompson was sent out to prevent this traffic, and we venture to assert that not one syllable is said on the subject in his instructions, and if he had those instructions, we would ask if he acted in pursuance of them when he took the American brig *Tremont* as a prize, loaded with lumber, and how much of the treaty between the United States and Mexico he fulfilled, when he required the Captain of the *Tremont* to come on board the *Correo* with his papers, while that treaty expressly provided that a Mexican armed vessel shall board an American Merchantman by sending one of her officers on board, with not more than three men, and shall in no case require the Captain of the Merchantman to leave the vessel with his papers.

That negroes were imported into Texas from Cuba, and even from Africa direct, at this time, is generally conceded; Fannin, the Texas martyr, was himself accused of importation of African slaves by

---

a blockade of the Brazos, and that he attacked the *Tremont* for violating the blockade. See sworn statement of A. J. Yates, I. N. Moreland, and A. C. Allen in *Texas Republican*, September 19, 1835.—Editors of QUARTERLY.

no less a man than S. Rhoads Fisher, later Secretary of the Texan Navy.[1] This version of the matter might also account for the great anger of the Americans at Anahuac, who may have been awaiting the arrival of a slaver, in order to purchase their wares and cross over the Sabine with cheaper negroes than could be purchased in the United States. In favor of this theory is the note which Bancroft[2] inserts without comment that "Washington Stiles, one of the crew of the *Tremont,* in the trial of Thompson at New Orleans for piracy, swore that Thompson said that if he could capture two American vessels, the *Tremont* and the *San Felipe,* his fortune would be made and he would stop." Just how his fortune would be made by capturing a vessel loaded with lumber, as the *Tremont* was, is not clear, but if it was loaded with two or three hundred negroes selling at one dollar a pound, his statement looks reasonable, as there was an active demand for negroes at this price. The *Tremont* was captured September 1, but Thompson's previous acts had so exasperated the Texans that they had already determined to seize the *Correo* and accomplish his downfall.

It was in pursuance of this design that the Texan trading schooner *San Felipe* arrived off the mouth of the Brazos, September 1, just as a prize crew from the *Correo* was weighing anchor on the *Tremont.* The *San Felipe* was purchased in New Orleans for Texas by Thomas F. McKinney, a prosperous merchant of Quintana, and associated at that time in business with Samuel M. Williams. The price paid for the vessel was $8,965 "including freight on board when taken,"[3] which would lead one to believe that the purchasers were in a great hurry indeed, not to have time to unload the freight,—unless said freight consisted of holloware (cannon) as Edward states, and was such goods as they wanted. Captain William A. Hurd was put in command.[4] Captain Thomp-

[1]Broadside (December 17, 1835), "To the People of Texas," in Dienst, Collection of Documents (cited henceforth as Dienst, Col. Doc.), II, 23; see below p. 24; Eugene C. Barker, in QUARTERLY, VI, 152.

[2]Bancroft, II, 161, note 23. Bancroft is here quoting from Winthrop, *Report of the Trial of Thomas M. Thompson,* 3, 16, which I have not seen.

[3]Dienst, Col. Doc., II, 16.

[4]Edward, 249.

son of the *Correo* was aware of the intentions of the *San Felipe* and was keeping a sharp lookout for her, and seemed in no way disposed to evade her attack.[1] At 8 o'clock in the evening the *Correo* came up, and without warning fired into the *San Felipe*.[2] Bancroft says the fight lasted only three quarters of an hour. The *Texas Republican*,[3] which gives the best of the meager accounts, says:

On the arrival of the Schr. San Felipe, Capt. Hurd, at the bar of the Brazos, she was attacked by the piratical schooner Correo, Capt. Thompson, and after an engagement of two hours the Correo made off, but was pursued, overtaken and captured by the San Felipe and brought back. The officers and crew consisted of Captain T., 1st and 2d Lieutenants and 14 seamen. During the engagement one of the crew of the Correo, a native of Baltimore named Blackburn, received a mortal wound, of which he died two days after. Capt. Hurd took command of the Correo and departed for New Orleans, with the pirates in chains, leaving Capt. Grayson in command of the San Felipe to follow.[4]

The *San Felipe* had a very short career after this engagement. I can find no further mention of her in any history; but Edward Hall says in a letter to Stephen F. Austin that the *San Felipe* went in pursuit of a Mexican armed vessel and was lost in Matagorda Bay, that the heavy cannon had been saved and was on Bird Island, and that he had heard from Matagorda that the schooner *William Robbins* sailed from there on the 13th with the intention of picking up the gun and taking it to the Brazos.[5] It seems, however, that the *San Felipe* was only aground, and not wrecked. In a letter addressed to the General Council by Thomas F. McKinney, dated November 11, he stated that they succeeded in getting the schooner off, and that, in company with the *William Rob-*

[1] Letter from J. W. Fannin, Jr., in Dienst, Col. Doc., II, 23.
[2] Yoakum, II, 162. Edward, 249, claims that the *San Felipe* was hailed, and that she replied with shot, and thus fired first. This is merely an assertion.
[3] Issue of September 19, 1835, in Austin Papers; *cf.* Bancroft, II, 162.
[4] In the *Telegraph and Texas Register*, October 15, 1837, Captain Thompson states that the steamboat *Laura* assisted in this capture. Bancroft (II, 162) says: "An engagement followed, which lasted for three-quarters of an hour, when Thompson drew off. In the morning the *San Felipe*, taken in tow by a small steamboat, the *Laura*, went in pursuit of the *Correo*, which was almost becalmed about six miles off. The Mexican captain surrendered without further fighting."
[5] Hall to Austin, November 23, 1835. Austin Papers.

bins she would go at once to New Orleans. He said that on last Thursday, while the *San Felipe* lay on the beach, she exchanged several shots with a Mexican vessel, and he thought that some shot hit the Mexican, which put to sea.[1] Nothing further can be found relative to her, except a resolution of the General Council of January 17, 1836, by which R. R. Royall was appointed agent to take charge of and secure the wreck of the schooner and whatever belonged to her, then lying on the beach in or near Paso Cavallo and report to the Government.[2]

Meanwhile, Captain Thompson and his Lieutenant O'Campo were carried to New Orleans and in January, 1836, they were tried on a charge of piracy in the Federal District Court, the suit being termed, "The United States vs. Thompson."[3] New Orleans sympathy was largely with Texas, and the excitement seems to have reached the attorneys on both sides. P. Soulé, one of Thompson's attorneys, and H. Carleton, United States District Attorney, passed the lie between them, and threw at each other inkstands, books, etc., for which Judge Harper of the United States District Court sentenced them each to six hours imprisonment. The jury sat on the case one whole night, and brought in a verdict to acquit O'Campo. It was not able to agree in Thompson's case, and the court ordered a new trial. Mr. Carleton thereupon, with leave of the court, entered a *nolle prosequi,* and the prisoners were discharged.[4]

The *New Orleans Courier*[5] said concerning the trial. "The issue of the suit . . . is indeed a very remarkable one—such, it may be said, as never happened before—the pirates set at liberty and the Attorneys committed to jail." *The Commercial Bulletin*[6] gave the following account of it:

[1] *Proceedings of the General Council,* 10.
[2] *Ibid.,* 346.
[3] *The Courier,* January 14 and 16, 1836; *New Orleans News* of various dates—all in Dienst, Col. Doc., I, 5.
[4] Yoakum (I, 356) says Thompson was acquitted. This is not so; an acquittal would imply that the *San Felipe* had erred in capturing him, which a withdrawal of the charge does not necessarily imply. Thompson had a bad case to defend, as he could not produce his commission at the trial; but it is to Mexico's credit that she nevertheless sustained him.
[5] In its issue for January 16, 1836.
[6] For January 18, 1836.

On Saturday last, the Judge of the United States District Court of this city, having ordered the commitment of the District Attorney and of Mr. Soule, in consequence of an altercation which took place between those gentlemen during the trial of Thomson, a large number of the friends of the District Attorney visited him during his short confinement.

While they were assembled in the room where the District Attorney was confined, Dr. Archer, one of the Commissioners from Texas, addressed Randell Hunt, Esq., the assistant Counsel of the District Attorney in the trial of Thomson, in a very eloquent manner, expressing his own satisfaction and that of his fellow-citizens of Texas, for the able and powerful address of Mr. Hunt delivered to the Jury in that cause, and for his bold and righteous vindication of the cause of Texas in her present struggle for Civil Liberty, and concluded by saying that his fellow-citizens could give no adequate compensation to his efforts, and his expression of those sentiments, but they desired his acceptance of some testimonials of their approbation and esteem. He then presented Mr. Hunt in the name of the Citizens of Texas, with a very splendid Gold Lever, the most valuable that could be found in this city, engraved inside the case, with the following inscription: "Presented by the Citizens of Texas to Randell Hunt, Esq., in testimony of their esteem of his exalted talents, and eloquent vindication of the cause of *Truth, Justice and Civil Liberty.*" This, with a very superb cane and some other valuable jewels, were received by Mr. Hunt, and on receiving them with a letter, which we have inserted below, he made a very appropriate and eloquent reply.

New Orleans, Jan. 16, 1836.

Randell Hunt, Esq.

Dear Sir—The undersigned respectfully request your acceptance of the enclosed, as a slight testimonial of their personal esteem, and an expression of their admiration of the able and eloquent address delivered to the Jury by yourself last evening—of your powerful effort in the cause of truth and Justice, and last, not least, the warm and heartfelt expression of your sympathies for their oppressed and struggling country and your righteous vindication of their conduct in the present crisis. That the most brilliant success may attend your career, and the talents and learning which you possess ever be engaged in as just and holy a cause as the one you have so eloquently sustained, whether it be to shield the innocent, or punish the guilty—and that you may reap a rich reward in your own heart, and the approbation of your fellow citizens, is the sincere prayer of

Your obedient servants,

Adolphus Storm [Sterne],	B. T. Archer,
W. H. Bynum,	S. F. Austin,
John A. Wharton,	W. H. Wharton,
A. Hotchkiss,	W. G. Logan,
Wm. Bryan,	J. Scott,
A. C. Allen,	A. J. Yates.

New Orleans, Jan. 17, 1836.

Gentlemen—I acknowledge with the deepest sensibility, and the most unfeigned thanks, the receipt of your letter, and of the testimonials which accompany it.

When I consented to act with the District Attorney in the prosecution of Thompson, I did so with a single regard to the principles of truth, and justice, and liberty, and in the expectation of receiving no other reward than the consciousness of an honorable effort to serve my country on that occasion, to the best of my abilities. Judge then of my surprise, pleasure and pride I have experienced at the thanks, commendation and kindness heaped upon me by you all of whom are gentlemen of the highest respectability for private worth, and many of whom are destined to fill some of the brightest pages of the history of these times; it is an honor of which the most distinguished man of this age might well feel proud.

If the defence of the principles of liberty be, as I feel assured, one of the highest duties of the profession to which I belong, I shall never cease to rejoice that that defence, in connection with the cause of Texas, became a part of my duty on the occasion to which you have adverted. A native American, I cannot but feel the deepest interest in the success of a people, connected with us by the ties of a common origin, and a common regard for equal rights, and bravely struggling for constitutional liberty. God speed the noble work!

Accept, gentlemen, once more my acknowledgements for the testimonials of esteem with which you have honored me, and re-

The Navy of the Republic of Texas. 9

ceive in return my best wishes for your individual happiness, and the welfare of your country.

I am, gentlemen, very respectfully,

Your obedient servant,

RANDALL HUNT.

To Messrs. B. T. Archer, etc.

Thus happily and amidst rejoicing, was closed the incident of the *Correo* and the *San Felipe*.[1]

II. ORGANIZATION OF THE NAVY.

At a mass meeting held at Columbia, August 15, 1835, a committee of fifteen persons was appointed to prepare an address to the municipalities of Texas, asking them for co-operation in a call for a consultation of all Texas. The address requested that each municipality should elect five delegates to meet at Washington, on the 15th of October. On this date only thirty-two members were present; these not being sufficient for a quorum, the meeting was adjourned to November 1. By the 3rd of November fifty-five members had assembled at San Felipe instead of Washington. This consultation was authorized to organize a government, and to provide ways and means for carrying on the war. A provisional government was formed, in which Henry Smith was appointed governor and James W. Robinson lieutenant governor.[2]

One of the very first matters receiving the attention of the Consultation was the proper protection of the sea coast. As it was impossible to create a navy in a day, it was determined to issue letters of marque and reprisal; and it was hoped that by having numerous privateers cruising upon the Texas coast, not only would Texas be protected, but the Mexicans would be seriously harassed. It will be sufficient for the purposes of this narrative merely to outline the plans proposed and those finally adopted. On the 31st

---

[1] About two years afterward, August 17, 1837, Capt. J. D. Boylan, commanding the Texan man of war *Brutus*, captured the *Correo* again. She was then passing by the name of *Rafaelita*. (See *Texas Navy Papers*, State Library.)

[2] Bancroft, II, 162, 169, 171; *Journals of the Consultation*, 50.

of October, 1835, the General Council, which was looking after the interests of Texas until the opening of the Consultation, issued letters of marque to several "gentlemen of the lower country."[1] I am of the opinion that these commissions were not used, or were surrendered later, and those authorized by the Consultation accepted in exchange. The first application for "letters" to the Consultation was made on November 8th, 1835, by A. C. Allen,[2] Mr. Allen proposed to "arm, man and fit out a vessel mounting nine guns, and fifty stand of small arms, with fifty volunteers on board and four months provisions, to cruise off our coast as a privateer." The committee to whom this proposal was referred reported: "That they view the protection and defence of our seaboard of the greatest importance in the present crisis;" and recommended that Allen's proposal be accepted; that all authority vested in the Consultation be granted to him to cruise with such vessel as he might think proper to arm and man as a privateer; that a suitable commission be issued to him for that purpose by the executive; and that "the thanks of the convention be tendered to Mr. Allen, for his patriotism and devotion in our struggle for constitutional liberty." Further on it will appear that Mr. Allen made good use of the commission. Some one about this time must have raised the question as to the right of the Consultation to issue letters of marque; for on November 13th we find the following report on the subject from a select committee, of which D. C. Barrett was chairman:[3] "This convention, in adopting the declaration of the seventh of November, have organized this power, and by the provisions of the resolution constituting a provisional government, have vested this authority in the governor and general council; consequently these[4] requires no further action upon the subject by this house during its present session." Article four of the plan of the Provisional Government as finally adopted, authorized the governor "by himself, by and with the consent of the

[1]Report of General Council to Consultation in *Journals of the Consultation*, 11. For form of commission see THE QUARTERLY, VII, 278.
[2]*Journals of the Consultation*, 25-26.
[3]*Ibid.*, 40.
[4]There.

The Navy of the Republic of Texas. 11

council," to employ the army and navy in "all proper ways" for the defense of the country.[1]

The Council which was to assist the governor in the management of the navy was elected by the Consultation from its own membership, one from each municipality.[2] The Consultation adjourned on November 14, and the Governor and Council were now in power. On November 15, D. C. Barrett and A. Houston reported to the Council among other things that, "The Mexican Schooner Montezuma, with another vessel, is cruising in the Gulf. The Vera Cruzana is off Matagorda—more commissions for vessels in the Texas service are requested."[3] This information was derived from a letter from McKinney and Williams to the Consultation, dated the 9th. It has been affirmed that the letter was written to hurry the Council into issuing letters of marque, and that no Mexican vessels were then endangering the Texan coast. If this was the object, it served the purpose. The *Vera Cruzana* was the vessel that was said to have exchanged shots with the *San Felipe* as she lay on the beach in Matagorda Bay, as was mentioned in the last chapter.

On the next day, November 16, Governor Smith sent a message to the Council, one paragraph of which is as follows:

I recommend the granting of Letters of Marque and Reprisal; by doing which we cannot only prevent invasion by sea, but we can blockade all the ports of Mexico, and destroy her commerce, and annoy and harrass the enemy more in a few months, than by many years' war, carried on within our own limits. My own mind is satisfied that the whole of our maritime operations can be carried on by foreign capital and foreign enterprise. Already applications for commissions have been made; they are willing to take the hazard, as such afford them every encouragement.[4]

The governor here seems optimistic, but much that he anticipated from privateers came to pass. Not all who applied for commissions actually fitted out privateers; perhaps they did not like

---

[1]*Journals of the Consultation*, 44.
[2]*Proceedings of the General Council*, 3.
[3]*Ibid.*, 8.
[4]*Ibid.*, 13.

the restrictions which the commissions imposed. At this time the governor did not seem to think it necessary to form a national fleet; later, as privateers did not materialize according to his hopes, he viewed favorably the creation of a navy to be owned and controlled by Texas.

This message of the governor was referred to the committee on naval affairs, composed of Messrs. Perry, Harris, and West. On November 18 the committee reported themselves in favor of granting letters of marque under the following restrictions: (1) Applicants should be men of character and skill as naval tacticians, and no license should be granted to vessels under eighty tons burden, or carrying less than four twelve pound carronades, "or their equivalent in metal." (2) Cruising should be restricted to the Gulf of Mexico, and prizes made only of vessels sailing under the flag and commission of the central government of Mexico. (3) All prizes should be brought into ports of Texas and adjudicated by competent tribunals; and twenty-five per cent of the prize money should be paid into the public treasury, and the balance to the captors. (4) All persons cruising under license must give good security for the correct performance of the conditions mentioned in their commissions. (5) Commissions were not to be issued for more than six nor for less than three months, and were in any case to cease at the conclusion of war between Texas and Mexico. The report concludes as follows:

Your committee would further most earnestly represent that the establishment of a small Naval force for the security of our extended coast and the protection of our own commerce would seem to them highly necessary and indispensable, and under that conviction would recommend the purchase, arming, and equipping two schooners of twelve, and two schooners of six guns each, to cruise in, and about the bays and harbors of our coast. This arm of the service should be confided and entrusted only to men whose nautical skill and experience are well known and established, and whose activity and efficiency would with greater certainty secure the objects of its creation and organization.[1]

Here we have the first official recommendation for a navy to be entirely controlled by the government, and to consist of government vessels.

[1] *Proceedings of the General Council*, 25-27.

On the next day, November 19th, the Council took up the report of this committee. The first section was adopted; the second was amended to allow privateers to cruise on the high seas as well as in the Gulf; the third was amended to give the government only five, instead of twenty-five, per cent of the money derived from prizes; the fourth was stricken out; the fifth was agreed to without change; and then the entire report as amended was adopted.[1]

On the 19th, the committee on Naval affairs introduced an ordinance "for granting letters of Marque and Reprisal, and for the establishment of a Navy," which with a slight amendment was passed to its second reading.[2] The next day Governor Smith, who was not yet informed of this action, sent in a message in which he said, "Commissions granting letters of Marque and Reprisal, have been earnestly solicited, both by our own citizens and foreigners, and as yet have not been acted on." This subject, with others mentioned in the message, the governor deemed "of the most urgent and vital importance," and he thought that it should receive prompt attention.[3] Three days later, November 22, the Council met on special call of the president, and the ordinance for granting letters of marque and reprisal and for establishing a navy was taken up and read a second time. It was amended by inserting between the words "Texas" and "that" the following, "that the Governor, by and with the advice and consent of the Council, shall have power to grant letters of Marque and Reprisal," which was agreed to. On motion the rule in this case was suspended and the ordinance was read the third time and passed finally.[4] It was sent to the governor for his approval, and on the 24th he returned it with the following remarks:

To this bill I am bound to object as it now stands. The privileges granted to privateers seems to me rather unbounded—that this Government takes all the responsibilities without any interest in the captures which may be made.

If prizes are brought into our ports, the Government will be at the expense of adjudication and sale, without remuneration, pro-

[1]*Proceedings of the General Council*, 31.
[2]*Ibid.*, 32.
[3]*Ibid.*, 37-38.
[4]*Ibid.*, 44-45.

vided they should be found lawful prizes; if not lawful prizes they will be bound to make remuneration for the act of their commissioned agents, who have brought into our ports prizes which cannot be condemned and sold as such. Besides, I consider, agreeably to the provisions of the ordinance, that privateers would have an unbridled license to roam at large, without being particularly under the control of the Government, and kept within limits calculated to protect our own commerce, and might, in the end, be productive of more injury than good. . . . If they are not commissioned in a manner calculated to promote the public good by annoying our enemies and protecting our own commerce, they might prove injurious to the Government rather than an advantage. . . .

As it respects that part of the bill making provisions for the creation of a Navy. If it should be made out in a separate bill for that purpose, it would appear much better, and would entirely meet my views, as I deem it entirely necessary for the protection of our commerce. . . . I would therefore suggest the propriety of separating the substantive matter of the bill, and introduce one solely for the purposes of creating a Navy on proper principles, and leaving out the provision for granting letters of marque and reprisal, unless your honorable body may think proper to introduce it in a different shape. I am well aware that no good could result from granting commissions as contemplated by that portion of the bill and as such object to it.[1]

On the same day the ordinance was reconsidered. When the question was put, "shall this ordinance now pass? the veto of the Governor to the contrary notwithstanding," the vote stood three for passing and eight for rejection, so the ordinance was lost. It was recommitted, on motion, to the standing committee on naval affairs, and Mr. Westover was added to the committee.[2]

The next day, November 25, the committee presented an ordinance for granting letters of marque, which was read the first time; and, on motion, the rules were suspended, and it was read a second time. Mr. Hanks moved that the words "twenty per cent" be stricken out, and the words "ten per cent" be inserted, which was agreed to. The rule was further suspended, and the ordinance read a third time and passed. At the same time an ordinance for establishing a navy was introduced and by suspension of the rules

[1]*Proceedings of the General Council*, 51-52.
[2]*Ibid.*, 53.

hastened through its third reading and passed.[1] On the 26th, these two ordinances were reported enrolled.[2] The governor affixed his signature to the ordinance granting letters of marque and reprisal on the 27th of November, 1835.[3]

The ordinance granting letters of marque agreed in substance with the report of the committee on naval affairs as amended by the Council,[4] except that the government's share of prize money was increased in accordance with the governor's suggestion. Hanks's amendment to change that share from twenty per cent to ten per cent must have been overlooked when the ordinance was enrolled; for I have one of the original commissions,[5] and also one of the original copies of the supplementary letter issued a few days later, and the commission places the government's share of prize money at "twenty per cent." A few days afterwards, the ordinance was modified by further action of the governor and Council. Major Samuel Whiting called on the governor and stated that he was on his way to New Orleans, and wished there to fit out some privateers; and, as he did not know whom he would get to command them, or just what vessels he would secure, he wanted some blank commissions. So, on the 29th of November, Governor Smith in a message to the Council recommended the passage of an ordinance authorizing the executive to vest Whiting with authority to fill out the blanks, under special instructions from the executive in conformity therewith. A committee was appointed to draft such an ordinance and reported "an ordinance and decree supplemental to an ordinance and decree for granting letters of marque and reprisal, passed 25th November, 1835," which was laid on the table. On taking the matter up later the Council so amended the ordinance as to grant three blank

[1]*Proceedings of the General Council*, 55.
[2]*Ibid.*, 56.
[3]*Ordinances and Decrees of the Consultation*, etc., 23-24; a copy with autographs in Dienst, Col. Doc., II, 1.
[4]See pp. 12-13, above.
[5]This commission is printed on heavy paper by Baker and Borden, the date of the imprint being San Felipe, November 27, 1835. It bears the autographs of James W. Robinson, lieutenant-governor and *ex-officio* president of the Council; E. M. Pease, secretary of the Council; Henry Smith, governor; and C. B. Stewart, executive secretary.

commissions to Thomas F. McKinney and Silas Dinsmore to be filled for the same purpose; and, on motion of Mr. Hanks, it was further amended so as to provide that ten per cent of the prize money should be paid to the provisional government, anything to the contrary in the previous ordinance notwithstanding. The ordinance was then passed finally.[1] Whiting was allowed six blank commissions; McKinney and Dinsmore three.

Section 2 of this supplemental ordinance is interesting as making the first reference to a flag for the service:

Be it further ordained and decreed, etc., That all vessels sailing under Licenses, as Letters of Marque and Reprisal, which have been, or may hereafter be granted by the Governor and Council, or by the Governor, as provided in this supplementary Ordinance, or under any register or license of this Government, shall carry the flag of the Republic of the United States of Mexico, and shall have the figures 1, 8, 2, 4, cyphered in large Arabics on the white ground thereof.[2]

Under the ordinances whose history has been given, privateering commissions were granted as follows: To S. Dinsmore, Jr., and to Robert Potter, who later became secretary of the navy, on December 1; to Ira R. Lewis and other owners of the schooner *William Robbins,* on December 5; and to Benjamin F. Smith, on December 6. The minutes of the Council for December 6 show that there was also issued, on that day, a blank commission to the committee of safety for Matagorda, to be filled in for the captain of the *William Robbins;*[3] but this seems to have been a repetition either of the action or of the record concerning the same subject on the previous day. This was the last commission of the kind granted by the Council and Governor Smith. A month later, January 7, 1836, they seem to be sorry they ever granted privateering commissions at all, as the following request would indicate: "On motion of Mr. Barrett it was ordered that the committee on Naval affairs, be requested to examine into the expediency of retracting all letters of marque and reprisal heretofore granted by this

[1] *Proceedings of the General Council,* 73, 74, 75, 76. I have one or the original commissions given to McKinney and Dinsmore.
[2] *Ordinances and Decrees of the Consultation, etc.,* 38; original commission, Dienst, Col. Doc., II, 1.
[3] *Proceedings of the General Council, passim.*

Council," and Mr. Barrett was added to the committee for this special case.[1] On January 9 the committee reported progress and asked leave to sit again, which was granted;[2] but nothing further is heard from it. Two days later, January 11, Governor Smith made his severe charges against the Council, and in the excitement caused by his impeachment the subject seems to have been neglected till the Convention met.

The first constitution of the Republic conferred on Congress the power to grant letters of marque and reprisal.[3] A proclamation by President Houston, dated September 15, 1837, declares that all letters of marque and reprisal granted under authority of the Texan government had been recalled, but that the practice of granting them is renewed from the time when the proclamation is made public. This was because John A. Wharton, who had landed at Matamoras under a white flag in order to effect the exchange of his brother, William H. Wharton, then a prisoner in Mexico, had been arrested and detained.[4] On November 2, 1837, a joint resolution was passed by Congress endorsing the action of the president, and requesting him to grant commissions immediately to all applicants who would comply with certain stated conditions. No one availed himself of this opportunity; although the government, by the resolution, reduced its share of the value of prizes to two and one-half per cent. Congress ordered the letters of marque to be advertised in the *Telegraph*, which was done.[5]

I have purposely followed the granting of letters of marque through 1837, in order finally to dispose of the subject. As no action followed the various pronunciamentos, they savor a little of the Mexican style of conducting war. This remark does not apply of course to the first half dozen commissions issued, and which were actually used.

I have written at length on the subject of letters of marque, because such privateers as were fitted out proved of assistance to Texas in the beginning of her struggle, in giving the government

[1]*Proceedings of the General Council*, 275.
[2]*Ibid.*, 286.
[3]See Art. II, Sec. 4.
[4]*Telegraph and Texas Register*, September 16, 1837.
[5]*Ibid.*, September 23, 1837.

and the people a feeling of security from invasion by sea by means of transports convoyed by one of the two or three Mexican vessels then plying in the Gulf. Moreover, the captures made were very helpful at this critical time, and the privateers deserve no little credit for the help they afforded the Republic of Texas in her infancy. Just how great that help was we shall see at the proper time. Another reason for treating this subject at such length, is that it has been almost totally ignored by historians; and in my judgment, having so much to do with the beginnings of the Texas of to-day, it is deserving of a prominent place in the history of the State. But one writer that deals with Texas has any comment to make on the granting of letters of marque and reprisal, by the struggling colonies. This comment is so inconsistent and odd that I give it. It is characteristic of the man who penned it. His book is valuable for the facts it contains; but when he goes beyond facts his prejudices are so strong against the Texans that his judgment is warped. He says:

The second way in which the Provisional Government tried its hand at robbing was in granting letters of marque and reprisal. It passed two acts with this object, by the first of which (Nov. 27), it was provided that twenty per cent of the proceeds of the prizes should be paid into the treasury; by the second (Nov. 30), the amount was reduced to ten per cent. In thus authorizing individuals to fit out privateers, it could plead the precedents of the best-established and most righteous governments.[1]

He might have added that no nation ever had a more righteous cause, or was more in need of the assistance to be had only by the issuance of letters of marque.

As will be recalled, simultaneously with the issuance of an ordinance for granting letters of marque and reprisal, there was also passed on November 25, 1835, an ordinance establishing a navy. It is as follows:

[1]Gouge, *Fiscal History of Texas*, 27. Since the above was written another writer has mentioned letters of marque and reprisal in connection with the Texas Revolution. Eugene C. Barker, referring to them in *Political Science Quarterly*, XIX, 623, says: "At any rate, the matter is of little importance, for if any privateers were actually put in commission, nothing was ever heard of them." That this statement is erroneous will be demonstrated in the following chapter.

SEC. 1. *Be it ordained and decreed, and it is hereby ordained and decreed, by the General Council of the Provisional Government of Texas,* That there shall be, and there is hereby established a Navy, to consist of two schooners of twelve guns each, and two schooners of six guns each, with the requisite number of officers, seamen and marines for each schooner; and that the said schooners shall, as soon as practicable, be purchased, armed and equipped for warlike operations, offensive and defensive; and that they be put in commission and fitted out, and ordered into actual service; and the commander and officers of said Navy shall be under the orders and directions of the Governor and Council.

SEC. 2. *And be it further ordained and decreed, etc.,* That the Governor, by and with the advice and consent of the Council, shall nominate and appoint to the command of said vessels, officers of good character, courage and ability as naval tacticians. And the said vessels, when so fitted out, manned and equipped for naval operations, shall rendezvous in Galveston Bay, and the commanders thereof report to the Governor for further orders.[1]

I shall now relate the history of the various privateers sailing under letters of marque, or authorized by the needs of the hour to act as vessels of war in the defense of Texas. In doing this strict chronological order will be sacrificed to unity, and the history of each vessel will be followed separately to the end. This should avoid confusion, and make a more interesting and readable narrative. This course will be adhered to throughout the work wherever it seems to me best so to do. After the study of the privateers, the purchasing of the national vessels of war, their armament and officers and their various cruises will be considered, each receiving such space as its services entitle it to, and as material for its history has been found. The work of collection has been difficult, but I have found much that throws a new and clearer light on the services rendered by the navy, and its officers and men; and if I can add to their fame and that of their vessels by an impartial relation of the facts, the work I have undertaken will have served its purpose.

[1]Gammel, *Laws of Texas,* I, 931.

III. THE TEXAS PRIVATEERS.

The *William Robbins* seems to me, after careful search, to have been the second vessel fitted out by Texas, the *San Felipe* being the first. As noted in chapter I, the *William Robbins* was expected to accompany the *San Felipe* to New Orleans about the 10th of November, 1835. On the 13th of November we find her rendering her first service to Texas by transporting a heavy cannon, taken from the wreck of the *San Felipe,* from Bird Island to the Brazos.[1] Early in November, the Mexican vessels *Montezuma* and *Bravo* were reported to be blockading the Texas coast, and the committee of safety of the jurisdiction of Matagorda considered it important that a vessel should immediately be armed and equipped to attack and drive them off. The schooner *William Robbins* was at that time in the Bay of Matagorda, and by a resolution of the committee Ira R. Lewis and S. Rhoads Fisher were appointed to negotiate the purchase of this vessel for the Texas service. They concluded a bargain for her at thirty-five hundred dollars, but the money was paid by Thomas F. McKinney individually, in order that the government might have the option of buying and using her as a naval vessel.[2] She was placed under the command of William A. Hurd. On Thursday, November 19, 1835, it was reported in Matagorda that a schooner, which was afterwards found to be the *Hannah Elizabeth* from New Orleans, had been driven ashore at Paso Cavallo, pursued by a Mexican armed vessel. Early the next morning the *William Robbins,* in command of Captain Hurd, and with some citizens of Matagorda aboard, went to the assistance of the stranded schooner. On the evening of the 21st they anchored at the pilot house at the pass, and thus ascertained that the Mexican vessel had been driven by a norther to sea, and that the *Hannah Elizabeth* was in possession of a Mexican prize crew. Twenty volunteers from the *William Robbins,* together with Captain Hurd and three of his crew, were landed, all under the command of Captain S. Rhoads Fisher. When they presented themselves, the commander of the prize, Lieutenant Mateo, of the *Bravo,* delivered his sword, and surrendered himself

[1]Hall to Austin, November 23, 1835, Austin Papers.
[2]*Proceedings of the General Council,* 251.

and his eleven men as prisoners of war. Don Mateo stated[1] that the *Hannah Elizabeth* had on board fifteen Americans, and five Mexicans, besides a woman; that it had carried three cannon upon deck mounted, two sixes and a four; that its cargo included eighteen kegs of powder, and muskets and rifles. He said that, when he boarded her in the breakers at 7 p. m. with one boat and eleven men, not a gun was fired, nor the least resistance made; indeed, the cannon and small arms had been thrown overboard.[2] A number of the Americans and two Mexicans who claimed an interest in the cargo, Messrs. Carbajal and Fernando de León, were put on board the *Bravo;* from which Captain Fisher argues that they were great cowards. For Messrs. Kerr and the two Mexicans who were owners of the cargo, it could be said that their object in throwing over the cannon and muskets was to evade confiscation of the entire cargo for carrying contraband of war. Captain Hurd proposed that the cargo landed from the vessels be taken to Matagorda and sold. Peter Kerr, a passenger on board, who claimed a large amount of the goods, objected and wished to have them sold on the spot that he might purchase. Not knowing how soon the *Bravo* might return, this was agreed to, and Captain Hurd ordered the sale. As the men were not then prepared with money, their notes were taken, payable when they reached town. Kerr did not want his property sold, and proposed to pay as salvage fifty per cent on invoice cost. This was agreed to, and his part set aside, notwithstanding that he had no evidence of ownership. His part amounted to $2541. The balance of the goods was sold to various members of the expedition, and brought at auction $2843.83. Captain Fisher was publicly appointed agent by Captain Hurd, bills were made out, and notes drawn. On the 6th of

[1] A large printed hand-bill addressed "To the People of Texas," Matagorda, December 17, 1835. By S. Rhoads Fisher. Dienst, Col. Doc., II, 23. This version of this story of the *Hannah Elizabeth* I have accepted as the most reliable. While it is a personal vindication of S. Rhoads Fisher, and assails Governor Smith and particularly J. W. Fannin, Jr., it is attested on oath by leading citizens of Texas, and eyewitnesses of the entire transaction.
[2] V. M. Rose, *History of Victoria County*, 14, 111, 154, contains much information about the *Hannah Elizabeth*—"Her cargo of 500 muskets, two pieces of artillery, with a full equipment of ammunition valued at $35,000."

December Captain Fisher wrote an account, in accordance with the facts as narrated above, to R. R. Royall, a member of the Council. In this letter Captain Fisher asked the Council to adjudicate the matter; he said that the re-capture of the *Hannah Elizabeth* made it either a legal prize or the property of the salvors, and that he was the agent to represent either captors or salvors. It seems, however, that before Captain Fisher's letter reached the Council the governor had received another, severely condemning the whole proceeding. It was written by Col. J. W. Fannin, Jr.

To follow the history further, it will be necessary to return to the proceedings of the General Council. As already noted, a letter of marque was granted to the owners of the *William Robbins* on December 5, 1835.[1] On December 11, J. W. Fannin, Jr., addressed a letter from Matagorda to his excellency, Governor Henry Smith, and the General Council,[2] which agrees with Rhoads Fisher's statement, and gives further details. He says that one of the *Bravo's* parties in passing from the schooner in its small boat was capsized in the breakers, and with difficulty got on board again; while their boat drifted ashore and was discovered by a man named Somers and two companions. "They immediately got possession of the boat and with their firearms kept it, and prevented the Mexicans from retaking it, and by this means prevented an escape to the Bravo of the whole party, who had been ordered to rob, and afterwards burn and desert the schooner. In the meantime, a party from this town was got up, and proceeded below with the schooner *William Robbins,* recently purchased and armed for the public use. S. Rhoads Fisher commanded the marines, and Captain Hurd, recently of the schooner *San Felipe,* the crew of the *William Robbins.* . . . When said party landed and marched across, they found Somers and party walking their regular rounds, having kept up a guard for about *two days,* the lieutenant and crew having previously agreed to surrender, when an *officer* should appear to receive his sword, and thus save Mexican honor." Fannin then makes insinuating charges against

---

[1] Or December 6; see *Proceedings of the General Council,* 109, 114. *Cf.* p. 16 above.

[2] This letter I find only in Fisher's hand-bill, "To the People of Texas." See p. 21 above, note 1. The minutes of the Council and the Governor's message merely refer to it.

Captains Fisher and Hurd, and claims that the sale was a very dishonest one. After reading this letter, Governor Smith, without hearing anything from the other side, sent a scathing message to the Council,[1] asking it to look into and sift the matter. He referred to those who took part in the transaction as "bone pickers, who are eagle-eyed, ever hovering around to pounce upon their unfortunate prey," and said that he was "well aware of the intrigue, management and downright roguery, which has been universally practiced by the unprincipled speculators."

The letter was referred to a committee, which on December 17 made a report, accompanied by an ordinance to sequester and secure the cargo of the schooner *Hannah Elizabeth,* and advising that commissioners be appointed with power to seize and sequester the schooner, arrest persons, and suspend the commission of the commander of the *William Robbins,* if the facts in the case justified such a course, and report to the Council.[2] The report was adopted, and three commissioners were appointed. On December 22, R. R. Royall presented letters on the subject from J. G. Robertson and S. Rhoads Fisher to the Council,[3] which were placed on file. On January 3, 1836, Governor Smith transmitted to the Council the report of Thomas Barnett, one of the commissioners, which was referred to the Committee on State and Judiciary.[4] The next day the committee reported a request that two new commissioners be appointed to act with Barnett in place of the two originally appointed, but their report was tabled.[5] On January 7 it was brought up again and the addition of another commissioner to the three already appointed was recommended.[6] The explanation of this is that some of the commissioners who had been appointed either were not in Texas or would not act.[7]

This is the last we hear of the *Hannah Elizabeth* in the General Council or from the governor. The quarrel between the Council

[1]*Proceedings of the General Council,* 167-168.
[2]*Ibid.,* 168, 172-173.
[3]*Ibid.,* 193.
[4]*Ibid.,* 249.
[5]*Ibid.,* 254.
[6]*Ibid.,* 271, 272.
[7]Papers of the "Provisional Congress," Department of State, File 3,

and governor occurred soon after, and the report of the *Hannah Elizabeth* committee was left on the table. S. Rhoads Fisher, however, did not let the matter drop. He was very angry and wrote Colonel J. W. Fannin, who made the charges against him, a fiercely vituperative letter, charging him with being "incapable of adhering to the first principles of either . . . discretion or *truth*," and with bringing from Africa slaves whose "native lingo yet betrays their recent importation." The letter contained an implied invitation to Fannin to reply with a challenge. He was, however, too busy with his share in the campaign that was just then opening to turn aside for a private quarrel, and a few weeks later came his death at Goliad.[1]

Both Fisher and Fannin were in error; the latter in making his charges without sufficient examination or foundation, the former in taking Fannin to task too severely for the charges. At the worst, they implied nothing but a sharp business speculation, possibly not according to law. While they were disproved by Fisher, he was not justified in going to the length he did in his letter.

I have purposely dwelt at length on the *Hannah Elizabeth*, the *William Robbins*, and Captains Hurd and Fisher, because Yoakum, Thrall, the *Proceedings of the General Council*,[2] and other authorities or sources, mention the charges and even comment in a derogatory way, without mentioning the defense. As a further and final proof that the transaction was not a swindling affair, Captain Hurd was soon after this made an officer by the General Convention of Texas, and placed in command of the government vessel *Brutus*.[3] S. Rhoads Fisher was made chairman of the naval committee at the same time by the General Convention, and later on was secretary of the navy. No vindication could better testify to their character and proper conduct in the case in question than this elevation at the hands of their fellow-citizens.

Nearly twenty years later Peter Kerr was reimbursed by the

---

[1] Fisher to Fannin, January 12, 1836, in Fisher's Broadside "To the People of Texas." Dienst, Col. Doc., II, 23.
[2] Yoakum, II, 38; Thrall, 219; *Proceedings of the General Council, passim*.
[3] Gammel, *Laws of Texas*, I, 891.

"mixed commission" of the United States, for his loss in the *Hannah Elizabeth*. As the prisoners taken by the *Bravo* and *William Robbins* were about equal in number, on December 27, 1835, the Council requested the governor to correspond with the commanding officer at Matamoras, with a view of exchanging.[1] Nothing further is to be found regarding an exchange, but that the United States government claimed the credit of releasing all the prisoners except the captain of the *Hannah Elizabeth,* through the agency of their consul stationed at Matamoras.[2] The *Bravo* we do not hear of again until about April, 1836, when she was one of three Mexican vessels which engaged the Texan man of war *Independence* in a drawn battle. The New Orleans newspapers of July, 1836, mention that she was lost while on her way from Matamoras to Vera Cruz, and all on board perished with the exception of Captain Thompson and two marines.

As to the *William Robbins,* negotiations were at this time being carried on by the Council for her purchase, with the object of making a national war vessel of her. These negotiations were satisfactorily concluded, and she became the Texan war vessel *Liberty.* It seems worth while briefly to recount them here. The commissioners to the United States appear to have bought, or to have believed they had bought, the *William Robbins* (the name of which they changed to the *Liberty*) while on their way to New Orleans.[3] But there must have been some misunderstanding about the matter; for, on January 3, 1836, a communication was laid before the Council from Thomas F. McKinney, offering the *William Robbins* for sale to the government,[4] and the Committee on Naval Affairs recommended that an agent be appointed to examine the vessel with a view to purchasing. The report of the committee was adopted by the Council,[5] and on January 5th a decree was passed appointing Edmund Andrews and Wm. P. Harris agents to examine the *William Robbins* and the *Invincible,* and providing

[1]*Proceedings of the General Council,* 215.
[2]See *National Intelligencer,* February 14, 1837.
[3]See *Proceedings of the General Council,* 277; Austin, Archer, and Wharton to Smith, January 10, 1836, in the Diplomatic Correspondence of the Republic of Texas, State Library.
[4]*Cf.* p. 20 above.
[5]*Proceedings of the General Council,* 251-252.

for their purchase if the report was favorable.¹ Governor Smith approved of the ordinance with the exception of the provision for sending agents to purchase the *William Robbins*. As she had already been purchased by the commissioners to the United States, acting under the governor's instructions, in pursuance of a decree of the Council,² he did not want to create confusion by refusing their purchase of the vessel for the government.³ Notwithstanding the governor's protest, the ordinance passed without amendment by a constitutional majority on the 8th of January; but Governor Smith never signed or returned it, as is noted in the ordinance itself.⁴ This is the last we hear of the purchase of the *William Robbins* in the Council; for on the 11th of January the Governor made his famous charge against the Council, and everything was sidetracked for his impeachment and trial. However, as the *William Robbins* became the *Liberty,* it is fair to presume that the purchase by the commissioners was accepted as legal and binding; and when we later take up the study of the *Liberty* as a national war vessel, we shall be but completing the history of the *William Robbins,* privateer.

The third Texan privateer was the *Terrible,* commanded at different times by Captain John M. Allen, later mayor of the City of Galveston, and by Lieutenant Randolph. The *Terrible* sailed under a letter of marque procured on the 8th of November, 1835, by A. C. Allen, as already related.⁵ Little of her history is known, save that she patrolled the Gulf, and by her watchfulness, if not numerous prizes, made herself helpful to Texas. From the New Orleans papers⁶ I find that while cruising she was taken in charge by the United States war vessel *Boston,* and carried to Pensacola; but the offense with which she was charged having been committed on waters beyond the jurisdiction of the court, she was turned over to John H. Holland, Esq., marshal of this district of Louisiana. These charges were: 1st, that the *Terrible* was fitted out at New

¹*Proceedings of the General Council,* 263; Gammel, *Laws of Texas,* I, 1031.
²*See Ordinances and Decrees of the Consultation,* etc., 52-54.
³*Proceedings of the General Council,* 277-278.
⁴Gammel, *Laws of Texas,* I, 1033.
⁵See p. 10 above.
⁶Clipping in Dienst, Col. Doc., I, 25. The clipping is probably from the *New Orleans Bee* of date not earlier than October 1, nor later than October 5.

Orleans to wage war against a government with whom the United States was at peace; 2d, that the commander, Lieutenant Randolph, had manifested the intention of committing an act of piracy upon a Sardinian vessel, the *Pelicana Mexicana;* 3d, that he had sailed from this port without the authorization of the collector. She was discharged and soon afterward proceeded to sea. No particulars are given. From the *Telegraph and Texas Register*[1] and the brief comment of Lieutenant Tennison,[2] it is noted that under the command of Captain John M. Allen, the *Terrible* cruised up and down the coast of Mexico. During the cruise the *Terrible* captured between Sisal and Campeachy, the Mexican sloop *Matilda,* loaded with dry goods and provisions, and sent it into Galveston to be adjudicated. The last mention of her that I can find is by Tennison, who reports her off the Northeast pass of the Mississippi on the 12th of August, 1836[3] It is probable that when her commission expired she went into the regular coasting trade.

The fourth vessel to sail as a privateer in the Texas service was the *Thomas Toby,* previously the *De Kalb,* in the trade service between New Orleans and Texas. Her commander was Captain Hoyt. As in the case of the *Terrible,* little can be found concerning this vessel. Tennison calls attention to a cruise she made in October, 1836, in the following words:

[1]For August 16, 1836.
[2]Tennison's Journal, entry for August 11, 1836; in Dienst, Col. Doc., VI, 326. The Tennison Papers, which are the most valuable materials for the history of the first Texas navy that I know of, came into my possession by purchase. My attention was first called to them years ago by the late Judge C. W. Raines of the State Library at Austin. By copies of official documents sent me from the Naval Library of Washington, D. C., through the kindness of Secretary Long and Librarian Rawson, I was enabled positively to prove the papers to be Tennison's. Wm. A. Tennison entered the Texas naval service in the beginning of the navy, 1836, and remained with it to the last, having the honor to deliver the remnant of the Texas navy to the United States authorities after annexation. His papers and journal are all in manuscript, and have never been used. The fact that he makes many references to other vessels and naval events than those with which he had to do directly, leads me to believe that he selected some of these outside materials from articles in the current papers of that period. Where Tennison later describes his own experience on board Texan vessels, his journal is no doubt in part a copy of the log books of the vessels; for officers were in the habit of keeping journals and copying log books. This, of course, can not be proved, since the log books of the first navy are all lost, and only parts of one or two of the second navy exist; but it seems certain.
[3]*Ibid.,* entry for September 3, 1836.

The Texan privateer Thomas Toby (late De Kalb) Hoyt commander has been cruising off the ports of Vera Cruz, Sisal, Campeachy, Matamoras, and Tampico, since the first week in October, and had captured, about the 12th inst a Mexican schooner, and sent her into Texas. She soon after run in towards the fort at the mouth of the river, and playing her "long tom" upon it for some time, without, however, doing much damage, except frightening the good people of the town nearly out of their wits, who supposing her to be the vanguard of the Texian navy turned out *en masse,* repaired to the fort and along the river banks determined to repel any hostile movement of the imaginary Texian fleet. The commander of the privateer soon after transmitted a chaleng to the commandant of Tampico requesting a meeting with any armed Mexican vessel which might be in port; but receiving no answer within a reasonable time, she stood off and spoke the Louisiana determined to capture all Mexican property she fell in with.[1]

The same writer in another entry says:

The *Thomas Toby* has just sent into Galveston harbor a very valuable prize, being a large fine brig, strongly built, and capable of being fitted out as a man of war, bearing guns heavier than any now in the Mexican Navy. She was captured on the coast of Campeachy and has on board 200 tons of salt. The Tom Toby when last seen was in hot pursuit of two Mexican schooners; this pursuit will undoubtedly prove successful, as "Fortune ever favors the brave." It is gratifying to reflect that our flag flaunts over one brave band, whose dauntless spirits delight to career with the "stormy petrel," over the tossing billows where danger lights the "Path to glory and to fame."[2]

In the early part of February, 1837, a mutiny was reported to have taken place on the *Thomas Toby* in which the doctor and purser were said to have been murdered. The mutiny was quelled, and the murderers lodged in prison in New Orleans.[3] The secretary of the navy in his report of September 30, 1837,[4] recommended the purchase of the vessel by the government; but before this recommendation could be acted upon, she was lost in the great storm off Galveston, in October, 1837.[5]

[1]Tennison's Journal, November 10, 1836.
[2]Tennison's Journal, Thursday, June 8, 1837. This capture of the brig loaded with salt is briefly noted by the *National Intelligencer*, August 2, 1837.
[3]*National Intelligencer*, February 25, 1837.
[4]Archives of the Department of State, Texas.
[5]Tennison Papers, 332.

Many years afterwards two cannon were found near Virginia Point, and identified as those belonging to the *Thomas Toby;* they were purchased by the Galveston Artillery Company. These particular cannon had been presented to Texas by the ladies of Havana, as the following letter indicates:

War Department, Columbia,
Dec. 3rd, 1836.

To Messrs. Thomas Toby and Bros.:

Gents. I am instructed by the house of Representatives of the Republic of Texas, to take necessary measures to procure two pieces of cannon (brass) which were presented by the ladies of Havana to the Republic. By a letter received by Messrs. Shriver and Grayson, it appears that they received from you on board the schooner Thomas Toby two brass cannons, and they are under the impression they are the pieces alluded to. You will please inform me as soon as possible if such is the case.

WILLIAM G. COOK,
Acting Sec't'y.

The *Thomas Toby* was named for the government agent of Texas in New Orleans.[1] It was said in a New Orleans paper that the vessel was commanded by Captain Suares.[2] I can find his name mentioned but once, and in no other place, and presume that he must have been the first lieutenant who temporarily had command; it is possible also that this was a typographical error for (Jas.) Sever, who later was lieutenant on the *Invincible.*

The *Flash,* Captains Luke A. Falvel, and Marstella, seems to have been the next privateer fitted out for Texas—under just what circumstances, and by whom I am unable to discover. On March 12, 1836, Falvel received his commission as captain in the navy from Robert Potter, and the crew was sworn in.[3] The *Flash* was ordered to proceed to the south of the Brazos, take on board all the women and children in that section of the country who were fleeing before the Mexican advance, in the "Runaway Scrape," carry them to Morgan's Point, at the head of Galveston Bay, and defend that place in the event of an attack. Upon this occasion

---
[1]Shipman, *Frontier Life,* 386.
[2]Clipping in Dienst, Col. Doc., I, 25. The clipping is probably from the *Commercial Bulletin,* but its date is uncertain.
[3]Ben C. Stuart in Galveston *News,* October 8, 1899. *The Proceedings of the General Council* do not mention Falvel.

the *Flash* had on board the two famous pieces of artillery known as the "Twin Sisters," which did such execution in the battle of San Jacinto a short time after; and upon arriving at Morgan's Point they were sent up to Harrisburg on the sloop *Opie*, Lieutenant Aaron Burns, and delivered to the proper officers. A short time after the arrival of the *Flash* at Morgan's Point the express rider for the Texas Cabinet, Michael McCormick, came in and reported that he was unable to find the Texan army, which was supposed to be on the retreat. Upon receipt of this intelligence, Captain Falvel was ordered to take on board all the families about the bay, and proceed towards Galveston Island. Accordingly there were embarked on board the *Flash* all the members of the Texan Cabinet who were at the Point, together with their wives and children. Among the number were Bailey Hardeman, secretary of state, his wife and two sons; Colonel Thomas, secretary of the treasury; Colonel Robert Potter, secretary of the navy; Mrs. Burnet, wife of President Burnet, and her son William; Lorenzo de Zavala and his three children. President Burnet declined to leave; and upon Captain Falvel's asking for instructions, he was directed to proceed at once to Galveston Island with the women and children, and defend the place if an attack were made. The next morning the vessel had proceeded down the bay to a point midway between Clopper's Point and Red Fish Bars, when President Burnet came on board in a small boat. On arriving at Galveston Island, the *Flash* came to anchor off the old Mexican customhouse, which stood near the corner of Avenue A. and Eleventh Street. The next day, April 20, the women and children were landed and the *Flash* proceeded to Fort Point, in order to defend the place if attacked by sea. During the trip there were about 150 persons on the little vessel. One historian[1] says that on April 26th "Most of the families of refugees were already on the schooner *Flash*, Captain Falvel, ready to sail for New Orleans, and had orders to sail that morning as Santa Anna was expected every day at the Island. The captain declined to attempt to cross the bar until there was a change of wind, and while waiting, the messenger, Col. Calder, arrived with the news of the battle of San Jacinto;

[1]Thrall, 521.

The Navy of the Republic of Texas. 31

this victory put a quietus on the terror stricken inhabitants of Texas who were fleeing the country." In May, 1837, the *Flash* was reported stranded on shore.[1] Whether she got off at this time and later suffered another accident, I cannot find out; but it is possibly to the same mishap that another writer[2] refers when he says that the *Flash*, under Captain Marstella, was lost at the west end of the island (Galveston), her captain having mistaken San Luis pass for the entrance to Galveston harbor. Among the special laws passed at the the extra session of the Tenth Legislature, number twenty-three, there is an appropriation of "$5022.21 to Luke A. Falvel for services as sailing master in the navy of the late Republic of Texas, and authorizing the comptroller to pay the same in the new issue of Confederate Treasury notes."[3] This is the last item that I have been able to obtain relative to the *Flash* and her commander.

The next armed vessel which assisted Texas, was the steamboat *Ocean*, Captain Grayson, the same who, as lieutenant, was left in charge of the *San Felipe*, as related in chapter I. This vessel was paid for mainly by the aid of subscriptions of citizens of Mobile, her equipment costing some five to eight thousand dollars.[4] It was on board the *Ocean* that the notorious H. A. Hubbell and the volunteers from New Orleans arrived on June 3 at Velasco,[5] and had Santa Anna taken to shore, as he was about to depart for Mexico, in conformity with the treaty entered into by him and the Texas government. In July, 1836, we find her again giving help to the Texas cause. The schooner *Brutus* was at Matagorda, blockaded by the Mexican brig of war *Vencedor del Alamo*, and she was expected to be relieved "by the sch's Invincible, Union, and other vessels that had gone there in tow of the steamboat *Ocean*, for the purpose of capturing the brig. The steamboat was laden with volunteers, and for her protection there was raised a breastwork of cotton bales.[6] She was successful in rescuing the

[1] *National Intelligencer*, May 30, 1837.
[2] Ben C. Stuart, in the Galveston *News*, October 8, 1899.
[3] *Texas Almanac*, 1865, p. 34.
[4] *A Vindication of the Conduct of the Agency of Texas*, a pamphlet by William Bryan, in Dienst, Col. Doc., II, 16.
[5] *El Correo Atlantico*, New Orleans, June 20, 1836. Thrall (547) calls her the "Ocean Queen."
[6] New Orleans *Commercial Bulletin*, July 18, 1836.

Brutus from her perilous position. As to what became of her later on, there are no data.

This finishes the last of those vessels that served as regularly commissioned privateers, and that can properly be termed Texan vessels, acting as a navy for Texas until her vessels of war were fully prepared to defend her coast. There were other vessels that aided Texas, notably the *Julius Caesar*, Captains Lightburn and Moore; the *Champion;* the *Flora;* the *Yellow Stone,* commanded by Captain Grayson; and other vessels that acted as transports for munitions of war and provisions, and in bringing volunteers to Texas. Since, however, their registers and papers emanated from the United States Government, and they were ostensibly in the trade between the United States and Texas, they can not be given a distinct place in a history of the Texas Navy. Nor did they win any great victory; but in the formative days of the new Republic the value of these small privateers to the government of Texas, in captures, and in protection of the coast was incalculable, and deserves honorable mention. Let not Texas in her present greatness despise the day of small things.

IV. NAVAL VESSELS BOUGHT AND EQUIPPED.

The navy of Texas became a reality in January and February, 1836, when four vessels of war were purchased. These were the *Liberty, Invincible, Independence,* and *Brutus;* and during 1836 and 1837 they comprised the total strength of the navy. The *Liberty* was the rechristened *William Robbins,* and we have already seen how the government acquired it.[1] At the same time that the purchase of the *William Robbins* was authorized (January 3) the naval committee of the General Council reported that "Messrs. McKinney and Williams, through Mr. Williams, have made a purchase of, and equipped a schooner of about one hundred and twenty-six tons burthen, adapted to the object of protecting our commerce against the enemy. This vessel, called the 'Invincible,' is now in the Bay of Galveston, and is generously offered to the Government of Texas, by the owners, at first cost and charges." The committee were of the opinion that the pro-

---

[1] See above, pp. 25-26.

tection of our own commerce, the destruction of that of the enemy, and the transportation of our supplies by water were of the highest importance, and made the possession of an adequate naval force indispensable; they therefore advised that "a suitable agent be appointed to examine the schooner 'Invincible,' and her equipments, and if suited to the objects of cruising in the Gulf, or about our coasts that an immediate purchase be made of the vessel." The report was adopted, and an ordinance making it effective was passed on January 5, 1836.[1] The same ordinance also adopted the United States naval regulations for Texas.

As has already been stated, Governor Smith did not believe that the Council should create confusion by meddling with a power delegated to the commissioners to the United States, and on January 6, he asked for the particulars respecting the *Invincible*.[2] This was the beginning of the quarrel between the governor and the Council; and so far as it concerns the *Invincible* we must follow it. On the 8th a committee to which had been referred the governor's message asking for information, reported that the ordinance which was now in his hands would furnish all the information necessary. At a special evening session the same day Mr. Barret offered the following resolutions:

Whereas, the Mexican sloop of war, Montezuma, is now reported to be in the bay of Galveston, and Texas is not in full possession of any vessel of sufficient force to meet her in action, and whereas the schooner Invincible is offered to the government of Texas, by Messrs. McKinney and Williams, upon terms which Government accepts, therefore,

Be it resolved, that a register of said schooner Invincible be made as the property of the Government, under he directions of the Governor, who is hereby authorized to execute the same, and give a duplicate thereof into the hands of Thomas F. McKinney, as evidence of the ownership of said vessel, and to retain the other on the files of the execuive office.

Be it further resolved, that the governor is advised and authorized to issue to Thomas F. McKinney, a letter of appointment as commander of the schooner Invincible, as a national vessel of war, removable at the pleasure of the Governor and Council, and in-

[1]*Proceedings of the General Council*, 250-252; Gammel, *Laws of Texas*, I, 1031-1033.
[2]*Ibid.*, 266.

struct said McKinney to take command of said vessel of war, and man and provide her for a criuse against the enemy, within the Gulf of Mexico or any of its waters, until further ordered.[1] . . .

The resolution was adopted, and a committee of two instructed to wait on the governor with the purpose of immediately carrying it into effect. Just what took place between this committee and the governor has never transpired, but the governor was greatly angered against the Council, as his message will prove. He evidently gained the impression that the Council was trying by foul means to drive him to do its will regardless of his own opinions. It will be recalled that he was hurried into granting letters of marque by the report that the *Montezuma* was endangering the Texan coast.[2] It was either a strange coincidence, thought the governor, that just as another law relative to the navy was being passed the *Montezuma* should re-appear, or that the men who wished to pass the bill recalled their former success in shouting "the wolf! the wolf!" and again raised the cry with the expectation of "railroading" the measure through. This must have been Governor Smith's belief when he wrote the message quoted in part below:

. . . You urge me by resolutions to make appointments, fit out vessels, as government vessels, registering them as such, appointing landsmen to command a naval expedition by making representations urgent in their nature, and for what. I see no reason but to carry into effect by the hurried and improvident acts of my department, the views of your favorite object by getting my sanction to an act disorganizing in its nature, and ruinous in its effects. Instead of acting as becomes the counsellors and guardians of a free people; you resolve yourselves into low, intriguing, caucussing parties, pass resolutions without a quorum, predicated on false premises, and endeavor to ruin the country by countenancing, aiding and abetting marauding parties,[3] and if you could only deceive me enough, you would join with it a piratical co-operation. You have acted in bad faith, and seem determined by

[1]*Proceedings of the General Council*, 282-84.
[2]See above, p. 11.
[3]This expression evidently refers to the Matamoras expedition. See THE QUARTERLY, V, 312 *et seq.*

your acts to destroy the very institutions which you are pledged and sworn to support. . . . Mexican like, you are ready to sacrifice your country at the shrine of plunder. . . . Base corruption has crept into your councils, men who, if possible, would deceive their God. . . . The appointment and instructions founded on the resolutions predicated on false premises, shall now be tested. I will immediately countermand the order made out in such haste, and as you say, and as her register says, the armed vessel Invincible is a Government vessel, I will immediately order a suitable officer of the Government to go and take charge of her in the name of the Government, and hold her subject to my order. And if that be refused, I will immediately recall her register by proclamation to the world. I would further suggest to you that our foreign agents have been commissioned and specially instructed to fill out our navy, and procure the proper officers and crews; and unless they can be certainly informed of the absolute purchase in time, to prevent their purchase of a similar one, the purchase so made by you, shall never be ratified or become binding on this Government; because you would do the Government serious injury by meddling with matters which you have put out of your power by special appointment.[1]

The governor closed his message by declaring the Council adjourned until March 1, and said that until then he would contrive to discharge his duties as commander-in-chief of the army and navy.

This message, naturally, created a sensation. The Council referred it to a committee which on the 11th reported resolutions deposing the governor and appointing Lieutenant-Governor James W. Robinson to take his place. The resolutions were adopted and an address to the people was issued by the Council presenting its side of the quarrel, but we will leave the matter here and resume the history of the *Invincible*.[2]

Lieutenant-Governor Robinson, in his message to the Council, January 14, 1836, said, "As a necessary and important measure that stands intimately connected with the defense of the country, and one to which I invite your attention, is the creation and due

[1] *Proceedings of the General Council*, 290-292.
[2] *Ibid.*, 294-302.

organization of a corps of marines, and as you have purchased two vessels for the public service, and shortly expect two more, to be purchased by your agents abroad, it would be very desirable to have that corps organized, and ready for service, with as little delay as possible."[1] On February 3, Governor Smith, who never acknowledged being deposed, issued to Thomas R. Jackson a warrant to demand certain papers from the Council, among them one showing "the terms on which the armed vessel Invincible has been tendered and accepted by the Government."[2] This is the last utterance of Governor Smith or the General Council relative to the *Invincible* and the navy.

On March 1 the General Convention superseded the General Council and brought order out of chaos. After the declaration of Texan independence, on March 2, 1836, the Convention turned to the formation of a constitution, and on the 9th a draft was reported which touched the subject of the navy as follows: Congress was empowered to "grant letters of marque and reprisal, and make rules concerning captures on land and water," to "provide and maintain a navy, to raise and support armies, and to make rules for the government and regulation of the land and naval forces;" the president was declared to be commander-in-chief of the army and navy; and judges of the supreme and inferior courts were given exclusive admiralty and maritime jurisdiction.[3]

Thursday, March 10, Mr. Carson stated "that he had received information of the arrival of the Brutus and Invincible, at the mouth of the river Brazos, destined for the service of the Republic of Texas; and that it was important to commission those vessels; he would, therefore, move that a select committee on naval affairs be raised, to inquire into and report in relation thereto. This was decided in the affirmative, and the president appointed Messrs. Potter, Everett, and Fisher of Matagorda."[4] On Sunday the 13th, the chairman appointed Messrs. Carson and Fisher, of Matagorda, a committee "to forward commissions, etc., to our naval

[1] *Proceedings of the General Council,* 325.
[2] *Ibid.,* 351-52.
[3] Gammel, *Laws of Texas,* I, 862, 863, 865.
[4] *Ibid.,* I, 881.

The Navy of the Republic of Texas. 37

commanders;" and the same day Mr. Carson introduced a resolution "That a standing committee of five on naval affairs be appointed to draw up and forward all necessary instructions and orders for the government of the officers of our navy." This was adopted; and the president appointed Messrs. S. Rhoads Fisher, Hamilton, Zavala, Gazley, and Carson. The next day Mr. Carson resigned from the committee and was replaced by Mr. Waller. At the same time the chairman, Fisher, reported that they had appointed and commissioned the following persons officers in the naval service of Texas, to-wit: "George Wheelright, Captain to schooner Liberty; Charles Hawkins, Captain to schooner Independence[;] Jerimiah Brown, captain to schooner Invincible; William A. Hurd, Captain to schooner Brutus; Arthur Robertson, Captain of marines." The report stated also that the committee had forwarded letters of instructions to said officers.[1] As this is our introduction to the two vessels *Brutus* and *Independence,* and as nothing further is to be found in the government proceedings concerning their purchase, we must seek elsewhere for the information, as well as for additional matter relative to the *Invincible.*

Besides the *Liberty, Independence,* and *Brutus,* the records of the period mention two other vessels in the government service. One of these, the *Cayuga,* was a small steamboat, commanded by Captain William P. Harris, and carrying two light guns. Apparently it did not belong to the government, but was impressed by President Burnet and ordered to the defence of Galveston Island, April 28, 1836.[2] After this emergency no more is heard of it. The other was the *Correo.* This was a Mexican vessel captured by the *Brutus,* August 12, 1837. She was apparently attached to the navy during 1837-1838, and in the State Library there is a list of her officers, but I have been unable to find that she performed any definite service for the country.

The *Invincible* was purchased in Baltimore by McKinney and

---

[1] Gammel, *Laws of Texas,* I, 890, 891, 892.
[2] *Texas Almanac,* 1869, p. 58. Those interested in studying conditions in Galveston at this period will find much valuable material in the archives of the Texas Historical Society of Galveston. The collection contains several hundred original letters of James Morgan and President Burnet. Through the courtesy of the secretary, Mr. E. G. Littlejohn, I was permitted to examine them.

Williams for $12,613.02, and they charged the government of Texas twelve and one-half per cent commission.¹ Besides this, General Thomas J. Green paid out of his private funds a considerable sum to fit her out, and William Bryan and Edward Hall, respectively general agent and purchasing agent for Texas in New Orleans, paid out $5,626.68 for the same purpose; making the total cost of the *Invincible* nearly $20,000.² At this time Thomas F. McKinney held a commission as her commander; but it was merely a nominal command, for he made no cruise. As already stated, the *Invincible* was of one hundred and twenty-five tons burthen, built in Baltimore, and originally intended for the African slave trade. She was a very fast sailer, slight in her construction, "clipper built," drawing about twelve feet of water, and originally calculated to sustain a battery. She carried two medium eighteens on pivots amidship, with two nines and four six-pounders in the waist, and was intended to have a crew of seventy. The *Liberty,* though smaller, being of some sixty tons burthen, was of stouter construction, carried four guns of small caliber, and was an ordinary sailer. The *Brutus,* of one hundred and twenty-five tons burthen, was a slow sailer, and carried eight guns. The *Independence* was of about the same description as the *Brutus*. It was fitted out by General Green in New Orleans, largely from his private funds, at the same time that he helped to equip the *Invincible.* The *Brutus* had been intended for the Texan service as early as December, but her departure was delayed by the petition of twenty-eight underwriters of New Orleans to United States District Attorney Carleton, claiming that she was being "armed with six cannon, and one large one on a pivot for the purpose of capturing Mexican vessels, which, with their cargoes are principally insured by the underwriters of this city." Carleton replied deploring the fact that they did not furnish him with affidavits and the names of witnesses in order that he might have something more substantial than rumors upon which to base legal proceedings, and promising to enforce the law

---

¹McKinney, *To All who may have Seen and Read,* etc. (pamphlet, Columbia, 1836), p. 10.
²*A Vindication of the Conduct of the Agency of Texas, in New Orleans* (pamphlet, 1836), pp. 12-18.

The Navy of the Republic of Texas.   39

when provided with the necessary evidence that a breach of it was contemplated.¹ After the *Brutus* had been offered to the Texan Government she was detained in New Orleans a while; but some time between January 23 and February 15, 1836, she arrived at Matagorda. This appears from a report made by the advisory committee of the Council to Acting Governor J. W. Robinson, on February 15, 1836.² The *Independence* was fitted out by the New Orleans agents at the same time as the *Invincible, Brutus,* and *Liberty*. Her cost was $5000 for the vessel, and some $5000 for outfitting.³

Having given as complete a history of the purchase and equipment of these vessels as our material permits, we will now follow each vessel in her various cruises, and note such events as are worthy of a place in a history of the navy of Texas. To the *Liberty*, which was the first vessel bought for the government, and whose career was the shortest and in its inglorious ending the saddest of all the fleet, will be devoted the following chapter.

V. THE LIBERTY.

While, as noted in the last chapter, instructions were being carried to Captain George Wheelwright, the newly appointed commander of the *Liberty*, Captain William S. Brown, intent upon a capture, was cruising on the high seas with the *Liberty*, seeking Mexican vessels. On March 3, 1836, he fell in with the *Pelícano*, a trading schooner, commanded by Captain Pérez.¹ The *Pelícano* was cleared from the port of New Orleans on February 25, 1836, by James W. Zachari, with a cargo purporting to consist of 550 barrels of flour; but in each barrel after the capture it was found that there were concealed three kegs of gunpowder intended for the Mexican army. The *Pelícano* was a Baltimore built vessel of the first class, carrying three large brass pieces, and having on board, besides her crew, twenty soldiers, double armed with muskets.⁵ As the *Liberty* carried but four small guns, she was really

¹*House Exec. Docs.,* 25 Cong., 2 Sess., No. 74, pp. 12-13.
²Papers of the General Council, file No. 433.
³*A Vindication of the Conduct of the Agency of Texas, in New Orleans,* p. 5. Pamphlet, p. 5, Dienst, Col. Doc., Vol. II, 16.
⁴*Commercial Advertiser,* New Orleans, April 25, 1836; undated clipping from the New Orleans *True American,* Austin Papers.
⁵*House Journal,* 3d Tex. Cong., 114.

venturesome to attempt the capture, especially as the fight took place within point blank range of the guns of the port of Sisal. Three of the *Liberty's* men, led by James O'Connor,[1] boarded the *Pelicano*. Before others could go to their assistance they killed seven marines, and caused several others to jump overboard, and the remainder to seek refuge beneath the hatches. The prize was manned with a crew and carried to Matagorda Bay, where she was wrecked in attempting to cross the bar.[2] The cargo, however, was saved. In landing, some of the barrels were stove in, and it was then that they were, upon examination, found to contain powder.[3]

It seems that Zachari and Company denied that the powder was on board the *Pelicano*. When this denial came to the knowledge of Captain Brown, he addressed the following letter to John Gibson, editor of the *True American*, a paper friendly to Texas:

GALVESTON BAY, May 8, 1836.
To the Editor of the True American.

SIR—By Capt. Appleton, I am informed that J. W. Zacherie denied that there was any Powder on board schooner Pelicano. I do assure you that there was 280 kegs—whether he knew it or not, I am not able to say. In addition to the above quantity, there were a number stowed in barrels of apples, potatoes, etc. I have found a number of letters on the Prize which proved the above fact. I feel it to be my duty to state these facts in regard to the Powder. There was no mention made of it on the manifest.

My situation requires that I should keep a constant lookout, and when I see the Mexican flag flying, I shall either take it or be taken. I can not fly from a Mexican, and will not.

Respectfully yours,
W. S. BROWN,
Commander Schooner Liberty. (Texian.)

In a proclamation of March 31, 1836, General Houston refers to the capture of the *Pelicano* as follows: "Captain Brown, with one of our vessels, has taken a Mexican vessel with 420 barrels of flour, 300 kegs of powder and other supplies for the army."[4]

[1]Archives of Texas, file 2424.
[2]*Telegraph and Texas Register*, August 18, 1838, Austin Papers.
[3]New Orleans *Commercial Advertiser*, April 25, 1836, Austin Papers.
[4]Proclamation to the people of the east of Brazos, March 31, 1836. Copy in an unidentified newspaper clipping.

From the date of Captain Brown's letter above, it is evident that he was in Galveston Bay May 8, 1836. Whether he relinquished the command of the *Liberty* at this time to George Wheelwright, who had been commissioned on March 12, there is no evidence to show; but from a short sketch of Brown, which afterwards appeared in the *Telegraph and Texas Register*,[1] he seems at about this time to have committed some act which caused Commodore Hawkins to order his confinement in irons, and for this he resigned. In the summer of 1836 President Burnet gave him another commission, with the express understanding that he was not again to be subject to the order of Commodore Hawkins. He went to New Orleans to get a boat and there died.[2]

It is very probable that in May or June, 1836, Captain Wheelright took command of the *Liberty*, but her next cruise to New Orleans was her last. She accompanied as a convoy the schooner *Flora* with the wounded General Sam Houston on board, and arrived at New Orleans May 22, 1836.[3] She was here detained on account of repairs, and in July was sold to pay the cost of them.[4] In the legislative halls of Texas we hear an echo of the *Liberty* in after years in the form of a petition from the captors of the schooner *Pelicano* for their share of the prize. The petition was favorably reported by the Judiciary Committee, whose report recites, among other things, that the district court of Brazoria county, which by law was invested with admiralty jurisdiction, had duly condemned the *Pelicano* and her cargo as lawful prize; that the value of the cargo of flour was $7584.05; and that half of that amount was due the captors.[5] The committee, therefore, recommended a joint resolution for the payment of their just share to the officers, crew, and marines of the *Liberty*. James O'Connor, the first man to board the *Pelicano*, was to receive an extra share.[6]

This closes the history of the *Liberty*, whose career, while brief,

[1] August 18, 1838.
[2] Captain William Brown was a younger brother of Jeremiah Brown, who was appointed captain of the *Invincible*.
[3] New Orleans *Commercial Bulletin*, May 23, 1836.
[4] Henry W. Morfit, Report, Velasco, Texas, August 13, 1836; in *Senate Docs.*, 24th Cong., 2nd Sess. (Serial No. 297), Doc. 20, p. 5.
[5] *House Journal*, 3d Tex. Cong., 114.
[6] Archives of Texas, file No. 2424.

was not unworthy of her name, save in her ending, which, if a reflection at all, is rather on her government than on herself.

VI. THE INVINCIBLE.

In Chapter IV the Invincible was left at the point where, on March 12, 1836, Captain Jeremiah Brown was appointed by the General Consultation to her command.[1] With his commission he also received orders to cruise along the coast and engage or drive off the Mexican war vessel, *Montezuma*. This vessel had so far done no great harm to the Texan interests, but since she was first reported off the Texan coast in November, 1835, shippers had lived in constant dread of her. After patroling the coast for some time, Captain Brown received a hint to search for the *Montezuma* near the mouth of the Rio Grande. He arrived there opportunely. An embargo had been laid by the Mexican government on all vessels in the port of Matamoras in order to prevent information reaching the Texans of an expedition which was being prepared to land two thousand men at Cópano Bay. The *Montezuma,* now rechristened the *Bravo,*[2] had just crossed the bar at the mouth of the Rio Grande, which is some thirty-five miles from Matamoras, and had lost her rudder. On the third of April, at ten o'clock a. m., while she was waiting to refit inside, the *Invincible* came in sight from the north. At 12 o'clock she came opposite, and Lieutenant William H. Leving, in a small boat, went on board the *Bravo*. The *Bravo,* becoming suspicious, slipped her cable and endeavored to retreat with Lieutenant Leving on board. A sharp engagement

---

[1] In the course of her career the following officers served for varying terms on the *Invincible:* Captains Jeremiah Brown and Henry L Thompson; Lieutenants F. Johnson,. William H. Leving, P. W. Humphreys, ———— Newcomb, James Perry, Harrie Hornsby, Randolph Lee, ———— Logan, James Mellus, and James Sever; Surgeons O. P. Kelton and Dunn; Purser F. T. Wells; Sailing Masters Daniel Lloyd and Abbott; Midshipmen Alf. A. Wate and Robert Foster; Boatswain ———— Smith; Gunner Fred Franson; Captain of Marines F. M. Gibson; Lieutenants of Marines F. Ward and ———— Brooks. This list, which is compiled from Tennison's Journal, the New Orleans newspapers, and *The Texas Almanac,* 1860-65, is as complete as I can make it.

Yoakum, II, 124, says that L. Brown commanded the *Invincible;* there was no Captain L. Brown, and Captain W. S. Brown commanded the *Liberty.* The *Texas Almanac,* 1860, p. 58, says that Captain I. B. Brown commanded the *Invincible;* this also is an error.

[2] The Matamoras correspondents of the New Orleans papers call the vessel the *Bravo,* but explain that it was formerly the *Montezuma.*

then took place. The *Bravo* could not be steered, and ran aground near the north beach, where she was almost completely wrecked by a broadside from the *Invincible*. The crew reached the shore in safety, carrying with them Lieutenant Leving. The *Invincible* sustained no damage, but Lieutenant Leving was shot as a pirate on April 14, 1836.

While the action was going on between the *Invincible* and the *Bravo*, at two p. m. the *Pocket* came in sight. This vessel was from Boston, commanded by Elijah Howes, who sailed from New Orleans on the 28th day of March, laden with a cargo, shipped by Lizardi and Company of that city, generally understood to be Mexican agents. Captain Brown captured the *Pocket* and sailed into Galveston, where it was detained. Captain Howes and some of his crew proceeded to New Orleans, where he filed with the United States district attorney a protest against the capture. This reads as follows:[1]

. . . at half past two o'clock P. M. saw two sails off the Brassos, St. Jago, which fired several guns each; . . . in a short time the schooner which carried the Mexican flag bore away and stood for the shore, and the other vessel tacked ship and stood for his brig, she being about three or four miles distant; . . . they kept this course and said vessel run a short distance to the windward and spoke them. . . . The captain answered he was from New Orleans, and bound for Matamoras. The schooner that made these inquiries, proved to be the Texian armed vessel Invincible, Brown, commander, who ran a short distance past them, and then tacked ship and ran close to the windward of them. That said schooner then sent her boat on board the brig, with orders to Captain Howes, to proceed on board the Invincible with his papers, which was accordingly obeyed; . . . Abbott, sailing master of said vessel,—with one officer and several armed men took charge of the brig, . . . [and] the Texian flag of 1824 was hoisted in its place at the main peak of the Invincible. . . .

The protest then recites that, after remaining at this point for two days, the two vessels sailed together, reaching the mouth of the Brazos after a voyage of forty-eight hours. On arriving at Galveston the next day, they were detained there until April 24, 1836, when Captain Howes and his crew received permission to sail for New Orleans. They were informed by the Texan authorities that the *Pocket* would be retained as a guard ship. Upon this

[1] An unidentified newspaper clipping.

Captain Howes told them that he would abandon her. This he did, losing cargo, freight, and passage money. He arrived at New Orleans on the tenth day of May, and noted this protest:

And thereupon these said officers, and especially the said master, did protest, and with them I, notary, at their request, do most solemnly and publicly protest:
First, against the winds and the waves and the danger of the sea generally.
Second, against the illegal capture and detention of the aforesaid vessel and cargo.

The *Invincible* was denounced as a pirate to Commodore Dallas, who was commanding a United States squadron at Pensacola, and he ordered the sloop *Warren* to capture her, which was done on May 1.[1] The *Invincible* was carried into New Orleans, and forty-six of the crew were imprisoned. Captain Brown was not on the vessel when it was captured. On May 4, the prisoners were called for trial; but witnesses for the prosecution did not appear, and the case was postponed until the 6th,[2] when it was taken up before Judge Rawle of the United States district court.[3] The lawyers for the defense were Messrs. Seth Barton, Randall Hunt, and O. P. Jackson. But four witnesses were examined. Three officers of the *Warren* testified that they had taken the *Invincible* on charges preferred against her by an insurance company of New Orleans that she had detained an American vessel. The court here adjourned until the following day, when the case came up again. No affidavits appearing, and no evidence being introduced to warrant a commitment for trial, the prisoners were discharged. The *Commercial Bulletin*[4] reviewed the case as follows:

. . We have never seen a finer collection of robust, and honest faced tars, than the prisoners, and in a good cause, we should ever hope, that they might prove invincible. . . .
The defense of the Texans was that the vessel was captured in Mexican waters for contravening the laws of the Republic, i. e. Texas, by having on board contraband goods, powder, etc., and for contravening the laws of Nations by having on board material of war for the use and advantage of Santa Anna, who was impatiently awaiting the same. . . . They also said the vessel

---
[1] *New Orleans Bee*, May 3, 1836.
[2] New Orleans *Commercial Bulletin*, May 5, 1836.
[3] *Ibid.*, May 7, 1836.
[4] *Ibid.*

was detained for examination, by reason of her having two of Santa Anna's spies on board, with plans and charts to aid in the downfall of Texas, which was proven. The captain not being able to read Spanish in which the invoices and correspondence were written carried her before the admiralty court of Texas, where the truth came out. The court finding the *Pocket* laden with contraband goods, purchased with Santa Anna's money by his agent Lizardi, condemned them as a lawful prize, paid the captain his freight, nine hundred dollars, and later dismissed the vessel as neutral.

Captain Brown now came forward and was arrested, but was immediately released and thus escaped the preliminary jail term which the crew suffered. The episode closed with a letter of thanks from the Texans in New Orleans to the attorneys for the defense for their efficient service, part of which is as follows:[1]

NEW ORLEANS, May 7, 1836.
To Seth Barton, Randal Hunt and O. P. Jackson, Esqrs.
Gentlemen: We the undersigned citizens of Texas, embrace this opportunity of expressing to you our most heartfelt gratitude, in behalf of the officers and crew of the Texian man of war schooner *Invincible,* that of our country and ourselves, for the very able, lucid and eloquent manner, in which you defended the noble and grateful crew, from the false imputation of piracy, brought against them by the secret Mexican influence of this city. . . .

If in some future day you should visit our beautiful land, which is destined to be one of the most prosperous and happy on earth, your reflection must be pleasing indeed, to know you were among the number who voluntarily contributed to our righteous cause.

THOS. J. GREEN,
Brig'r Gen. of the Army of Texas.
A C ALLEN
SAMUEL M. WILLIAMS
S RHOADS FISHER
JAMES POWER
EDWARD CONRAD
HENRY AUSTIN
EDWARD HALL
SAMUEL ELLIS
Ro. WILSON
T. G. WESTREN
D. C. BARRITT
WM. BRYAN, Texas Agent.

[1] New Orleans *Commercial Bulletin,* May 10, 1836.

All claims against Texas on account of the *Pocket* were finally settled by a convention between the Texan government and that of the United States, the ratifications of which were exchanged July 6, 1838. The amount agreed upon was $11,750, which was paid, together with accrued interest, July 6, 1849. The whole amount was $12,455.[1]

After her release the *Invincible* was used for coast defense. In June, 1836, she figured in another exciting incident. In accordance with the treaty of Velasco, concluded May 14, 1836, the Texan government determined to transport President Santa Anna to Vera Cruz, and for that purpose he had already embarked on the *Invincible*, when, on the 5th of June, General Thomas Jefferson Green arrived with volunteers from New Orleans in the *Ocean*, and forbade the *Invincible* to sail.[2] Whether or not it was for the good of Texas that Santa Anna was detained and whether or not the government could have prevented the detention, will always remain debatable questions; but it is in any case a fact that Texas violated a treaty in permitting it.

The Mexican navy at this time was ascertained to be lying in port, wanting men, arms and other equipment;[3] so the *Invincible* remained riding at anchor off the bar of Velasco, until July 4, when, as already related, she went to the relief of the schooner *Brutus*,[4] which was blockaded at Matagorda by the *Vencedor del Alamo*. This vessel had been dispatched from Vera Cruz to protect the Mexican schooners, *Comanche, Fanny Butler,* and *Watchman*, which were laden with provisions for the Mexican troops.[5] Finding that the Texans had already intercepted these vessels, and appropriated their cargoes, the *Vencedor del Alamo* very wisely returned to Vera Cruz.[6] There the *Invincible* finally found and

---

[1] For a more detailed account of the case of the *Pocket*, see the article by Mr. Neu in this number of THE QUARTERLY.—EDITOR QUARTERLY.

[2] See Williams, *Life of Sam Houston*, 218-221.

[3] New Orleans *Commercial Bulletin*, June 14 and July 13, 1836.

[4] See THE QUARTERLY, XII, 195. In the navy manuscripts of the Texas State Library are several letters dated Velasco, May 30, 1836, disclosing a serious misunderstanding between Commodore Hawkins and Captain J. Brown. Hawkins wished to remove Brown from the command of the *Invincible*, but he failed to accomplish his object.

[5] New Orleans *Commercial Bulletin*, July 18, 1836.

[6] The story of the capture of these vessels is extremely interesting. On the 29th of May, 1836, General Rusk ordered Major Isaac Burton, commanding a company of mounted rangers to scour the coast from the

The Navy of the Republic of Texas. 47

challenged her to battle, which was declined on the pretext that the crew of the vessel challenged were, for want of pay, not in a condition to fight. Later the *Invincible* fell in with a French vessel, and Captain Brown had to explain that he was not a pirate, but was sailing under the flag of Texas. The captain of the Frenchman was greatly surprised; for he had never heard of such a country, and did not know where it was; and he could not realize the fact of the creation of a new republic, not known to him.[1]

The *Invincible* now went to New Orleans; and after taking on board as passengers Branch T. Archer and William H. Wharton, she left, on July 13, 1836, for Galveston.[2] From here she cruised to Velasco, and about August 4[3] was ordered by President D. G. Burnet to New York for much needed repairs. She reached there in September, 1836. Unable to leave for want of funds, she might have been sold to meet expenses, but Hon. Samuel Swartwout paid her liabilities and let her go. She escaped arrest for violation of the neutrality laws of the United States only by running away from the vessel sent in pursuit of her. On March 14, 1837, she reached Galveston once more.

In the preceding October General Sam Houston had succeeded to the Presidency of Texas under the permanent government; and, in making his nominations to the Senate for commissions in the navy, he raised the list of officers to a number commensurate with the size of the navy. In April, by orders from the Navy Depart-

---

Guadalupe to Refugio. The company, though well mounted and armed, consisted of but twenty men. On the 2nd of June they received news of a suspicious vessel in the Bay of Cópano. By the break of day the next morning they were in ambush on the shore, and at eight o'clock, a signal was made for the vessel to send its boat ashore. Five men landed from the boat, and were promptly made prisoners. It was then manned by sixteen of Burton's rangers, who had no difficulty in seizing the *Watchman*. The vessel was ordered round to Velasco; but on the 17th, while it was still detained by contrary winds, the *Comanche* and *Fanny Butler*, also freighted with provisions for the Mexican army, anchored off the bar. The captain of the *Watchman* was made to decoy the commanders of these vessels on board his own, when they also were captured, and all three, with their valuable cargoes, were sent into the port of Velasco and condemned. From these bold achievements Major Burton and his rangers obtained the popular title of the "Horse Marines." The freight —worth $25,000—was of great service to the army.—*Telegraph and Texas Register*, August 2, 1836, and Yoakum, II, 160.

[1]*Telegraph and Texas Register*, August 16, 1836.
[2]*Louisiana Advertiser*, July 14, 1836.
[3]*Texas Almanac*, 1860, p. 163.

ment, Commander H. L. Thompson assumed the command of the *Invincible.* Accompanied by the *Brutus,* he first sailed in June to the mouth of the Mississippi; but, failing to find any of the enemy there, after a cruise of seven or eight days he turned to the coast of Mexico. On board with him was the Secretary of the Navy, S. Rhoads Fisher. The peculiar conduct of Fisher in abandoning his official duties at Houston to join in this cruise, he sought to justify in a letter to Dr. Bartlett, editor of the New York *Albion,* dated June 17, 1837, of which the essential part is in the following excerpt:[1]

It is ten days since I left Houston and immediately joined our little squadron, then lying in Galveston Bay, and after convoying the schooner Texas, ladened with Government stores to Matagorda Bay, up helm and bare away for Galveston, to receive orders from the President; we shall be there tomorrow, and shall stretch to the southward with the hope of falling in with the enemy. I am a volunteer. I can not precisely say amateur, but I have thought for some time upon the expediency of personally taking a part with the Navy, and have decided it was right. I know, you gentlemen of systematized governments will smile at the idea of the "Secretary of the Navy" turning sailor, and may be inclined to consider it better adapted to the adventure seeking disposition of the knight of the rueful countenance; but my opinion is that it will inspire great confidence in the men, and stimulate our Congress to do something for us; for it appears that this branch of national defense has never been popular in its infancy in any country; it ever has been compelled to fight itself into notice and government patronage; such at least I am satisfied is our case, and I think that my present step is precisely such as will suit the meridian of the views of our Texas population. We must be governed and actuated by such course as may best suit us; we are acting and legislating for ourselves and not for the world, and however at variance our system of policy may be with the preconceived ideas of right or wrong amongst the world at large, I humbly conceive that as we have to lie in the bed, we have the right to make it. Therefore, it is that however quixotic my present step may appear, and indeed for the United States or Great Britain would be, *I* am satisfied it is right.

In the course of this cruise several pirogues were captured at Mujeres Island. From them sails and provisions were obtained. In one was found a cargo of log wood, which the cap-

---

[1]See *Telegraph and Texas Register,* September 9, 1837.

The Navy of the Republic of Texas. 49

tain of the pirogue redeemed for $660 when they arrived at Sisal. This place was cannonaded by the Texans for three hours, but the attempt to take it was finally abandoned. The sailors and marines made repeated landings on this cruise and burned to the ground eight or nine towns. On one occasion Secretary of the Navy Fisher and Captain Boylan, then commanding the *Brutus,* landing with a few men and leaving their guns with their boat, strolled two or three hundred yards from the shore, when they were nearly captured by a small body of Mexican cavalry. Secretary Fisher used a pistol which he chanced to have with him and shot one of the Mexicans from his horse.[1] The Mexican fleet was meanwhile lying at Vera Cruz unmanned. Close to the Alacranes Island, the *Eliza Russell,* a British schooner in the Mexican trade, and the *Abispa,*[2] a Mexican vessel having on board a cargo transferred from the British schooner *Little Pen*[3] that had been wrecked on the island, were added to the list of prizes; but the *Eliza Russell* was soon released. The British government put in claims against that of Texas for damages on behalf of the master of the *Eliza Russell* and the owners of the cargo of the *Little Pen* amounting in the aggregate to about thirteen thousand dollars. The *Eliza Russell* claim—about four thousand dollars—was finally paid, but that of the *Little Pen* was not.[4]

Concerning the capture of the *Eliza Russell,* President Houston, in his message of November 21, 1837, expressed himself as follows:[5]

A circumstance [that] occurred during the last cruise which was directed by the executive, demands of me in this communication to notice the same to the honorable congress. Orders were issued from the navy department by direction of the executive, to the commander of the navy *that all neutral flags should be respected, unless the vessel was bound to an enemy's port, and*

---

[1]*Telegraph and Texas Register,* August 22, 1837, quoting the *Matagorda Bulletin.*

[2]Historians spell this name differently. Yoakum (II, 213) makes it "*Alispa*"; the *Texas Almanac,* 1860 (p. 164), "*Obispo*"; *Brown* (II, 127), "*Arispe*"; and Bancroft (II, 283), "*Avispa.*" Bancroft explains at length that *Avispa* means wasp in Spanish; and that therefore, "*Avispa*" must be correct. I use the variant form "*Abispa*," because it is this which appears in the documents I am following.

[3]This is the spelling invariably used by the British *chargé,* Elliot.

[4]For further details relative to the cases of the *Eliza Russell* and the *Little Pen,* see THE QUARTERLY, IX, 5-7.

[5]*Telegraph and Texas Register,* November 25, 1837; Crane, *Life and Select Literary Remains of Sam Houston,* 291.

had on board articles contraband of war. In violation of these orders, the Eliza Russell, an English brig was seized and sent into port, with a valuable cargo of fine goods, but containing nothing *contraband of war!* Upon information of the circumstances, the executive directed her immediate release, and the payment of damages, so far as he deemed it within his competency. The subject will be presented to Congress by the owner of the vessel, with a minute statement of all the facts. The circumstances of the case were immediately communicated to our commissioner near the court of St. James, and the executive has been assured that the despatch would reach England by the time of his arrival. Other acts connected with the cruise of a character not calculated to elevate us in the scale of nations, were done either without orders, or in direct violation of those which had been issued by the department.

By "other acts," President Houston probably meant S. Rhoads Fisher's absence from the seat of government, and the fact that the *Invincivle* overstayed the term of her sailing orders nearly two months. For this, and the illegal detention of the *Eliza Russell,* Fisher and Captain Thompson of the *Invincible* were suspended by the President from their duties until they could be tried. Fisher's trial took place before the Senate, and resulted in a resolution sustaining the president in his suspension of the secretary, and asking the latter, for the sake of harmony, to resign, while declaring at the same time that he was not found guilty of any crime or dishonorable conduct.[1] The department of the navy investigated the charges against Captain Thompson;[2] but it seems he was spared an earthly trial, for on November 1, 1837, he died. There was one solitary acknowledgment of his brave and splendid services for Texas, the record of which is as follows: "As a mark of respect to the memory of Captain H. L. Thompson, of the Texian Navy, who died this morning, on motion of Mr. Wharton, the Senate adjourned until 3 o'clock P. M."[3] Captain Thompson's experiences could hardly have failed to convince him of the truth in the old adage that republics are ungrateful.

On August 26, 1837, the *Invincible* and the *Brutus,* with the *Abispa* in tow, entered Galveston harbor. The *Brutus* entered the

---

[1]*Senate Journal,* 2d Tex. Cong., 1st and 2nd Sessions, 74-78, *passim;* Senate resolutions adopted November 28, 1837, Archives of Texas, 805.
[2]*House Journal,* 2nd Tex. Cong., 1st and 2nd Sessions, 170.
[3]*Senate Journal,* 2nd Tex. Cong., 42.

harbor with the *Abispa;* but, because of unfavorable conditions, the *Invincible* remained outside till morning, when she was attacked by two Mexican armed brigs, the *Vencedor del Alamo* and the *Libertador*. In coming to her assistance the *Brutus* ran aground and the *Invincible* continued the fight alone against both the Mexican vessels. Though both of these could outsail her, they would not risk an attempt to board, and were several times forced to draw away from close quarters. Finally, toward evening, the *Invincible* abandoned the struggle and undertook to enter the harbor; but in the attempt she also ran aground. The crew were saved, but during the night the vessel went to pieces.[1]

On May 23, 1838, President Houston approved a joint resolution authorizing the secretary of the treasury to pay to the officers and crew of the *Invincible* one-half of the proceeds of the prizes made by said vessel in her last cruise, which had been legally condemned.[2] This is the last official notice relative to the *Invincible*. Some of the officers and crew we shall find aboard other Texan vessels as we pursue our history. The *Invincible* did a great service for Texas, and her name should never be forgotten by those who love to give honor where honor is due.

VII. THE BRUTUS.

In the chapter devoted to the purchase of naval vessels a sketch was given of the *Brutus*—her armament, cost, and the officers appointed on March 12, 1836, to command her.[3] It was also there mentioned that she was intended for the Texan service as early as

[1]*The Telegraph and Texas Register*, September 2, 1837.
[2]Gammel, *Laws of Texas*, I, 1495.
[3]See THE QUARTERLY, XII, 201-203. At various times the following officers served on the *Brutus:* Captains L. C. Harby, William A. Hurd, and James D. Boylan; Lieutenants L. M. Hitchcock, ——— Lacy, John Damon, ——— Hoyt, G. W. Estis, J. G. Hurd, Osky Davis, ——— Mossat, Libel Hastings, ——— Dearing and ——— Galligher; Surgeon A. M. Levy; Purser Norman Hurd; Boatswain ——— Brown. Henry Riley served as an officer in some capacity, but his rank is unknown. Officers of marines were: Captain Arthur Robertson and First Lieutenant William Francis.

This list is compiled from Tennison's Journal, the New Orleans newspapers and the *Texas Almanac*, 1860, p. 165. In the list of the *Texas Almanac*, I. D. Bolan should be J. D. Boylan; I. G. Hurd should be J. G. Hurd; and it should be noted that Lieutenant Mellus did not serve on the *Brutus*. Brown, II, 127, writes "Boyland," and this is the spelling of the name in the Naval Papers of the State Library.

December, 1835. She was in the port of Galveston, when the *Invincible* arrived, on April 8, 1836, with her prize, the *Pocket*. She soon left Galveston, and after a short cruise stopped at New Orleans, during the trial of the crew of the *Invincible*. When the trial was over, Captains Brown and Hurd boasted that, from that time on, they would warn all United States vessels which they encountered beyond the jurisdiction of the United States against continuing their voyages; and that, if afterwards these vessels should be found doing so, they would be seized and condemned. As the Texas navy was unable to blockade the various Mexican ports and no distinction was made by Brown and Hurd between vessels with and without contraband of war, this was an idle and useless threat. A. J. Dallas, commanding the United States naval force in the Gulf of Mexico, was appealed to to convoy and protect American shipping,[1] and he assured the shippers that he would do so. This was eminently proper at the time, as no blockade of Mexican ports was then in force; but on the 21st of July, 1836, President Burnet issued a proclamation[2] from Velasco, declaring a blockade of the port of Matamoras, and ordering a sufficient number of war vessels to the mouth of the Rio Grande, and the Brazos Santiago to enforce the blockade strictly. Notwithstanding this effective blockade, which it was important for Texas to maintain in order to prevent transports laden with provisions reaching Matamoras from New Orleans, and transports loaded with troops at Matamoras from reaching Texas, Commodore Dallas, on August 9, 1836, wrote a letter from Pensacola,[3] stating that he would despatch a war vessel to the mouth of the Mississippi to convoy any vessels bound to Matamoras, and that he would raise the blockade. This, however, was an actual and legal, not a paper, blockade; and hence, in this case at least, Commodore Dallas was in the wrong and merited to the fullest extent the criticism directed against him by the Texans and the New Orleans press for his arbitrary interference with the struggling Republic of Texas.

On May 20, 1836, the *Brutus* left New Orleans to convoy ves-

[1] New Orleans *Commercial Bulletin*, May 11, 1836.
[2] *Telegraph and Texas Register*, August 16, 1836.
[3] The substance of this letter is quoted in the *Telegraph and Texas Register*, September 6, 1836, from the *New Orleans Bulletin*, August 13, 1836.

sels to Galveston. From Galveston she sailed for the Mexican coast and soon afterwards was, as has already been related, blockaded in the mouth of the Rio Grande by the Mexican brig of war, *Vencedor del Alamo*.[1] From this situation she was relieved in July, and soon thereafter was very effectually assisting, in her turn, in the blockade of Matamoras, as ordered by the proclamation of President Burnet.

The following item relative to the *Brutus* appears in a New Orleans paper the following month:[2]

Extract from the log-book of brig St John, arrived yesterday August 3d, in lat. 26 36, long. 87 25, was boarded by the first officer of the Texian armed schr. Brutus, Captain Hurd. The B. has been on a cruise for nearly three months, was in want of provisions—could not supply her with any article except sugar, being short. The officer told Captain Parmly, of the St. John, that the Brutus had a few days before taken a prize and sent her into Galveston—that she had on board $40,000 in specie, and a valuable cargo [?][3]

But a short time later, when the president wished to order a descent on Matamoras for the purpose of capturing military stores known to be there, he learned that Captain Hurd had, without orders, sailed for New York. Hurd's reason for this has never been ascertained.[4] While in the port of New York, between September, 1836, and February, 1837, the *Brutus* was in danger of being sold to defray her expenses; but, through the agency of Samuel Swartwout, she was freed from debt at the same time that he liberated the *Invincible*.[5] In March she sailed for Texas; and on the 15th of April, 1837, she again came to anchor in a Texas port, but without provisions and with the larger part of her crew missing.[6]

The *Independence* having been recently captured by the Mexicans, and the officers imprisoned, the Senate and House of Representatives, on April 29, 1837, passed a resolution instructing the

[1]THE QUARTERLY, XII, 195.
[2]The *New Orleans Bee*, August 10, 1836.
[3]The interrogation mark and the brackets belong to the original.
[4]D. G. Burnet, in *Texas Almanac*, 1861, p. 45.
[5]See p. 257 above.
[6]Proclamation of President Houston, May 5, 1837, in *Telegraph and Texas Register*, May 9, 1837.

president to send the *Brutus* and the *Invincible* to Brazos Santiago to negotiate an exchange of prisoners. On May 31, President Houston vetoed the resolution and in a lengthy message pointed out that there was nothing to gain and much to lose by sending the only two remaining war vessels on such an errand; that the prisoners would, on the approach of such vessels, very likely be carried to the interior, and treated more harshly; that any kind of a neutral or unarmed vessel would be better employed to carry such commissioners; and that, finally, he would veto the resolution, if for no other reason, because he considered it an unwarranted interference on the part of the legislative department with his constitutional authority as commander-in-chief of the navy.[1]

In June the *Brutus* cruised with the *Invincible* along the Mexican coast, with the secretary of the navy on board, as has been told already.[2]

In a letter describing this cruise to the secretary of the navy,[3] Captain Boylan says that on July 22 the two vessels captured the Mexican schooner *Union,* and a few days later the *Adventure* and the *Telegraph*—the former of which was burned, though the latter was sent into port for adjudication. On August 12 they captured the *Correo,* on the 17th the *Rafaelita,* which, as the *Correo Mexicano,* had been commanded in 1835 by Lieutenant T. M. Thompson, and soon afterwards the *Abispa.*

In a letter reviewing the cruise of the *Brutus* and *Invincible,* the secretary of the navy declared that their brilliant exploits were attributable to the skill, courage, and determination of the officers and crews; and that, if Congress would only extend its fostering protection and support to the navy, the names of Geo. W. Wheelright, Henry L. Thompson, and Jas. D. Boylan would "stand brightly conspicuous in the pages of our national history."[4]

What followed this hopeful prediction is an illustration of the irony of history; Captain Boylan was ordered by the acting secretary of the navy to superintend the collection of evidence concerning the charges preferred against Captain Thompson and the

[1] See *House Journal,* 1st Tex. Cong., 2nd Sess., pp. 84-87.
[2] See above, pp. 258-260.
[3] Boylan to Fisher, September 1, 1837, Navy Papers, Texas State Library.
[4] S. Rhoads Fisher to John Birdsall, T. J. Gazley and others, September 4, 1837, in *Telegraph and Texas Register,* September 9, 1837.

other officers of the *Invincible*,[1] while the president himself took in charge the head of the navy and secured his removal, as has been shown. In studying the records concerning the trial of these officers, one finds it difficult to believe that they were treated with justice. The one, without being found guilty, was dismissed from service; and what might have been the fortune of the other, but for the fact that death prevented his trial, must remain uncertain. The *Brutus* did much to help the Republic of Texas in its infancy, and they who served aboard her should ever be remembered by Texans with that degree of respect and admiration to which the heroic pioneers, be their services on sea or land, are entitled.

VIII. THE INDEPENDENCE.

In the study of the beginnings of the Texas navy the incidents connected with the purchase of the *Independence* have already been recounted.[2] On January 10, 1836, commanded by Captain Charles E. Hawkins,[3] she began her first cruise. From New Orleans she went to Galveston, and then proceeded along the Mexican coast, capturing and destroying a considerable number of small craft, with all material on board that could be used to the injury of Texas. Captain Hawkins, however, always respected the private property of the Mexicans. The *Independence* returned to New Orleans to refit, and soon after, March 12, 1836, Hawkins received his commission from the General Convention as captain of the *Independence*. He was senior captain of the Texas navy, and President Burnet, with the consent of his cabinet, appointed him commodore.[4] The *Independence* thus became the flagship of the fleet. Captain Hawkins was present at the seat of government

[1] *House Journal*, 2d Tex. Cong., 1st and 2d Sessions, 170.
[2] See THE QUARTERLY, XII, 202-203.
[3] According to Tennison's Journal, other officers of the *Independence* were: First Lieutenant Galligher, Second Lieutenant James Mellus, Sailingmaster W. P. Bradburn, Chief Surgeon A. Levy, Purser ―― Leving, Midshipmen William A. Tennison, and E. B. Harrington, Boatswain Robert Gyles, and Gunner George Marion. There was a crew of forty men. The Texas Almanac, 1860, p. 165, erroneously makes Galligher a Lieutenant on the Brutus. The Purser, Leving, was probably the same man as Lieutenant William H. Leving of the *Invincible*, who was detained on board the *Bravo*, and who was shot by order of Santa Anna in April, 1836. See pp. 6-7, above.
[4] See Burnet's Message in *Telegraph and Texas Register*, October 11, 1836.

when he was commissioned, and at once started for Matagorda to join his vessel for a cruise. On the 21st of March, in company with Captain William A. Hurd, he passed through San Felipe, and the editor of the *Telegraph and Texas Register*[1] said of them:

. . . The chivalry and determined character of these gentlemen is so well known that we are impatient to have them meet the force of the tyrant. Liberty and laurels will then waive over tyranny and defeat.

Arrived at Matagorda, Commodore Hawkins reorganized his corps of officers,[2] and March 20th the *Independence* started on her second cruise.

After destroying a number of small Mexican vessels during the earlier part of April, the *Independence* became engaged with two brigs of war, the *Urrea* and the *Bravo,* and an unknown schooner, of which the two brigs carried together twenty guns, while the *Independence* carried only eight. Before beginning the engagement, Commodore Hawkins asked his men if he should do so and was answered with cheers. He then made the attack, but the Mexican vessels soon drew off. The *Independence* then waited, expecting them to renew the fight; but they did not, and she sailed to Galveston, hoping to return with the *Invincible* and the *Brutus* and to capture the Mexican vessels.[3] The plan, however, was not carried out. The Texan government, believing that a descent upon

[1] Issue of March 24, 1836.

[2] In Tennison's Journal the following changes are noted: George Wheelwright was made Captain, James Mellus was promoted to the first lieutenancy, Frank B. Wright became second lieutenant, and J. W. Taylor, third. Thomas Crosby was appointed lieutenant of marines; Joseph Hill, an additional midshipman; William T. Brennan, captain's clerk, and J. T. K. Lothrop, supernumerary. All the rest of the officers of the first cruise except Lieutenant Galligher were retained for the second. But before the vessel sailed Mellus was ordered to the *Invincible;* Wright, Taylor and Lothrop became respectively first, second and third lieutenant, and Brennan became purser in place of Leving, who resigned. Captain Wheelwright was originally assigned with the *Liberty,* but at this time Captain Brown had that vessel off on a cruise.

[3] Tennison's Journal, folios 314-316. Tennison writes two accounts of this engagement, and one of them says that Commodore Hawkins was disappointed to find that the *Brutus* and *Invinvible* had, without his orders, gone to New York, which prevented his returning to the attack. This would fix the date of the encounter early in August. I have followed the account which is evidently the more accurate and which fixes it in April.

Galveston Island by the Mexicans was to be expected, detained the *Independence* to assist in the fortification of the island.[1]

While the officers and crew of the *Independence* were anxiously on the lookout from day to day, to be ready for the reputed invasion by sea, the battle of San Jacinto was fought and won by Texas on the 21st day of April, 1836. The news was brought to Galveston by Robert J. Calder, who had commanded a company in the battle, and Benjamin C. Franklin, who was judge of the admiralty court of the district of Brazos, but had fought as a private at San Jacinto. They made the trip to Galveston in a row-boat, and arrived on the 28th. Captain William S. Brown, of the *Invincible,* was the first to hail them with the question, "What news?" The account of what followed is taken from the historian Thrall, who had it from Calder himself:[2]

"When I told him, his men," says Calder, "literally lifted us on board, and in the midst of the wildest excitement Brown took off his hat and gave us three cheers, and threw it as far as he could into the bay. He then shouted to his men, 'Turn loose Long Tom.' After three discharges, he suddenly stopped and said: 'Hold on, boys, or old Hawkins (the senior commodore) will put me in irons again.'" Declining to wait for anything to eat, they were treated to the best liquor on the ship. They entered the captain's gig, and with four stalwart seamen started for the harbor. The Independence, the flagship of Commodore Hawkins, was anchored between them and the landing. As they approached the ship, Commodore Hawkins, with his glass, recognized Franklin and Calder, and began eagerly hailing for the news. When they were sufficiently near to be understood, a scene of excitement ensued beggaring description; and now it spread from vessel to vessel, reached groups on the land, and the welkin rang with shout after shout, until the people were hoarse. Hawkins fired thirteen guns. We suppose this was for the old thirteen colonies, as Hawkins had been in the U. S. navy. When the Commodore learned that they had been fasting for twenty-four hours, he had a sumptuous dinner prepared, and the party did not need much urging to stay and partake of the hospitalities of the old salt. They were staying a little too long, and finally Hawkins hinted that they had better go ashore and report to the President.

President Burnet, who was a great stickler for official prerogative, was a little miffed that everybody on the island should have

[1]Yoakum, II, 124.
[2]Thrall, 519, note.

heard the glorious news before he was notified of the battle and its result; and when the party reached the President's marquee they were received, as Calder says, "with stately courtesy—which at first we did not understand, thinking a little more cordiality and less formality would have suited the case and the messengers. This, however (continues our narrative) gradually subsided, and the president, before the interview closed, treated us with that grace and genial courtesy for which, throughout life, he was ever distinguished.

The president hastened to the battlefield; but having arrived there, he thought best to return to the coast. Accordingly, on the 5th of May he and his Cabinet and General Houston, with Santa Anna, Cos, and other Mexican prisoners, took passage on the *Yellowstone* back to Galveston Island. No accommodations being found there, Santa Anna was transferred to the *Independence;* and, when President Burnet and the Cabinet came on board, sail was made on the 8th for Velasco, at the mouth of the Brazos. Velasco was the great seaport of the Republic at that time. Arrived at Velasco, President Santa Anna entered into negotiations with his captors, which resulted in a treaty; and one of the stipulations was that he was to be sent to Vera Cruz to carry it into effect. We have already noted how he was taken from the *Invincible*,[1] which was to carry him and the commissioners to Vera Cruz.

Before this occurred, however, the *Independence* left Velasco for New Orleans. It reached that city in seven days, on June 13, and, below the Point, announced its arrival by Hawkins' favorite salute of thirteen guns.[2] Peter W. Grayson and James Collinsworth were on board as passengers. They were clothed with full power to negotiate with the United States Government for recognition of the independence of Texas, and left the next day for Washington for that purpose. The *Independence* cruised thence as far as the mouth of the Rio Grande, and for some reason, possibly for supplies, returned to New Orleans on August 3, 1836.[3] It reported the blockade of Matamoras an effective one, three Texan vessels being on guard.

On the 12th of August, the *Independence* spoke the schooner

---

[1] See above, p. 256.
[2] THE QUARTERLY, IV, 151, quoting from the New Orleans *Commercial Bulletin*, June 14, 1836.
[3] New Orleans *Commercial Bulletin*, August 4, 1836.

The Navy of the Republic of Texas. 59

of war *Terrible* at the northeast pass of the Mississippi, and informed that vessel that she was on her way to Matamoras to assist the *Invincible* in the blockade; when she arrived, however, the latter had left for New York. With the *Invincible* and the *Brutus* in New York, and the *Liberty* detained in New Orleans, Texas now found herself in momentary expectation of an invasion with only the *Independence* and four small privateers available for the defense of her coast.[1]

Toward the end of the year Commodore Hawkins again sailed for New Orleans to refit; and in January, 1837, he died of smallpox at Madam Hale's residence on Canal Street.[2] While he was only thirty-six years old at the time, he had had a varied experience, and had made a favorable impression upon every one with whom he came into contact. When a mere youth he entered the United States navy as a midshipman and was soon promoted to a lieutenancy; but, being of a restless disposition, on the outbreak of the Mexican Revolution he resigned his commission and entered the Mexican service with Commodore Porter with the rank of post-captain. Off Cuba he did excellent service and became a terror to the Spanish shipping. He resigned his position at the end of the revolution and in 1834 was a popular captain on the Chattahoochee River. In the fall of 1835 he joined Mexía's ill-fated expedition as *aide-de-camp* and after its failure came to Texas.[3] He presented himself to Governor Smith, and received from him the following letter:[4]

Executive Department of Texas.
To Stephen F. Austin, B. T Archer and Wm H Wharton, Esqrs—
Agents of the People of Texas to the United States of America.
Gentlemen

This will probably be handed you by Majr Charles E. Hawkins, a gentleman whose experience and ability in naval affairs would render his services acceptable in any govt—and more particularly in ours, which is just emerging from chaos. The zeal and patriotism with which Majr Hawkins has espoused our cause entitles him to the highest commendation. He has identified

---
[1]*House Journal*, 1st Tex. Cong., 1st Sess., 97.
[2]Tennison's Journal, folio 314.
[3]*Telegraph and Texas Register*, September 8, 1838; Yoakum, II, 39.
[4]Smith to Archer, Wharton, and Austin, December 20, 1835, in Austin Papers.

himself with us by taking the oath and performing the necessary requisites to become a citizen. I confidently hope that you will properly appreciate the worth and abilities of Majr Hawkins and assign him such duties in fitting out our Navy as his experience and abilities will warrant and also, such a command in it as his zeal patriotism and your better judgments may direct. I am Gentlemen,

Your obt servant
HENRY SMITH
Governor.

San Filipe de Austin, Dec 20, 1835

The commission appointed him to the command of the *Independence*. Soon afterward he was appointed commodore by President Burnet; and, holding that distinguished title at the head of a small but successful navy, he died in the discharge of his duty and in favor with his countrymen.

Owing to Commodore Hawkins's death, there were some changes in the official staff of the *Independence;* and, when she left New Orleans on what was destined to be her last cruise, April 10, 1837, George Wheelwright was captain, and John W. Taylor, J. T. K. Lothrop, Robert Cassin, and W. P. Bradburn were lieutenants.[1] A number of passengers were on board, among whom were Col. Wm. H. Wharton, minister to the United States, then on his return to Texas; Captain Darocher, Dr. Richard Cochran, and George Estis, a lieutenant in the Texas navy. They had smooth sailing until the morning of April 17, when the *Independence* was attacked by two Mexican war vessels; and after a running fight of four hours she was forced to surrender.

Texans who saw only the close of the fight, and were not acquainted with the details, conceived at first that the *Independence* had struck without a blow; and it was not until an official report of it was sent from Brazos Santiago by the officer in command, and corroborated from other sources, that the Texans would speak of the affair. The following sentiments[2] expressed the voice of the people before and after the official account arrived:

---

[1] Other officers were Surgeon Levy, Purser Brannon, Lieutenant of Marines Thomas Crosby, Midshipmen Wm. A. Tennison, E. B. Harrington, Joseph Hill, and —— Whitmore, Boatswain Robert Gyles, Gunner George Marion.

[2] *Telegraph and Texas Register*, June 8, 1837.

The Navy of the Republic of Texas. 61

We rejoice that we are at length enabled to furnish the official account of the capture of the Independence. We have hitherto forborne offering any comment upon the former vague accounts of this transaction, as we felt confident that many important facts had been overlooked which would completely exculpate our gallant tars from any disparaging imputation. We confess that when the first news of this combat arrived, containing the intellegence that the Independence had surrendered to two Mexican brigs without having received any injury, and her crew unhurt, a flash of shame and indignation mantled on our cheeks and the exclamation, "30 or 40 cowards and an old hulk are no loss," almost involuntarily fell from our lips; better we thought it would have been if this crew dauntlessly nailing this unsullied flag to the masthead, hurling their mortal defiance to the groveling foe—had fought on, and on, shouting the stern war cry of "victory or death," until the star of Texas, like the "star of day," went down in glory beneath the blood red billows, where foaming crests were singing to the last exulting cry of an unconquered band of freemen.

But the following statements have fully convinced us that we did injustice to these gallant tars, in harboring even for a moment a thought so unworthy of them and of the Texian name.

Far from blaming them for this surrender, we rejoice that they may yet be preserved to ride through the battle storm which shall rend the tyrant banner from the mast it disgraces. This desperate and protracted conflict will long hold a prominent place in the annals of Texas, and like the fall of the Alamo, it shall inspire our children with ennobling sentiments. No flush of shame shall redden their youthful cheeks as they read the page which declares that thirty-one Texians six only of these seamen, in a slow sailing armed schooner, mounting only six *sixes* and one long *nine* fought four hours and a half, two Mexican armed brigs, one mounting "16 medium eighteens" with a crew of 140 men; the other mounting "8 brass 12 pounders" and one long eighteen midship, with a crew of 120 men! One is astonished in reflecting that this little vessel was not annihilated by the first broadside from her powerful opponents, her dauntless little crew appear to have been preserved almost by a miracle, and it is cheering to reflect that their heroic conduct has furnished new proofs that our national escutcheon yet remains bright and untarnished. True, the flag of our country has once been struck on the stormy billows of the Gulf, but like the Roman eagle stooping before the sword of Epirus, it has wrung from the abashed conquerer the bitter confession, "Such men are invincible."

The official report[1] of the battle, written by Lieutenant J. W.

[1]*Telegraph and Texas Register*, June 8, 1837.

Taylor, who succeeded Captain Wheelwright in command after the latter was wounded, is as follows:

Brazos de St Iago April 21st 1837
To the Honorable S Rhoads Fisher, Secretary of the Navy

Sir—I have the honor hereby to transmit you an account of the late engagement between our government vessel Independence and two of the enemy's brigs of war, one the Libertador of sixteen eighteen pounders, 140 men; the other, the Vincedor del Alamo, mounting six twelve-pounders, and a long eighteen amidships, with one hundred men. Captain Wheelright having during the action received a very dangerous wound, the duty of sending this melancholy communication has devolved upon me, towit:

On the morning of the 17th, in latitude 29 deg. N., longitude 95 deg. 20 min. W., at 5 h. 30 m A. M. discovered two sail about 6 miles to windward; immediately beat to quarters; upon making us out they bore down for us with all sail set, signalized, and then spoke each other. At 9 h. 30 m., the Vincedor del Alamo bore away, getting in our wake to rake us, the Libertador keeping well on our weather quarter, we immediately hoisted our colors at the peak. The enemy in a few minutes hoisting theirs, the Libertador on our weather quarter edging down for us all the time, till within about one mile, gave us a broadside, without wounding any of our men or doing other damage; the fire was at the same time returned from our weather battery, consisting of three sixes and the pivot, a long nine, the wind blowing fresh, and from our extreme lowness our lee guns were continually under water, and even the weather ones occasionally dipped their muzzles quite under. The firing on both sides was thus briskly kept up for nearly two hours, the raking shots from the Vincedor in our wake nearly all passing over our heads, as yet sustaining but trifling injury; at 9 h. 30 m. the Libertador on our weather quarter, bore away and run down till within two cables length of us, luffed and gave us a broadside of round shot, grape and canister, while all this time the brig Vincedor in our wake continued her raking fire. Notwithstanding this we still continued on our course for Velasco, maintaining a hot action for full 15 minutes, with some effect upon her sails and rigging. The Libertador now hauled her wind, widening her distance, apparently wishing to be further from us, when she again opened her fire, which was on our part kept up without cessation. At 11 A. M. she again bore away, run down close to our quarter and gave us another broadside of round shot, grape and canister, which told plainly on our sails and rigging; as before she again hauled her wind to her former position, and played us briskly with round shot, one of which struck our hull, going through our copper and buried itself in her side. At 11 h. 30 m.

A. M. a round shot passed through our quarter gallery, against which Captain Wheelright was leaning, inflicted a severe wound on his right side, knocked the speaking trumpet out of his hand, terribly lacerating three of his fingers; he was conveyed below to the surgeon, leaving orders with me to continue the action. We still held on our course in our respective positions, keeping up an incessant fire, for full half hour, when the enemy signalized; then the Vincedor in our wake luffed up and gained well on our weather quarter; at that time the Libertador, on our weather beam bore away and ran down under our stern within pistol shot, our decks being completely exposed to her whole broadside, and at the same time open to the raking fire of the Vincedor on our weather quarter. In this situation, further resistance being utterly fruitless, and our attempts to beach the vessel ineffectual, I received orders, from Captain Wheelright to surrender, which was done.

The only damage done to our vessel, was that of parting some of our rigging, splitting the sails, a round shot in her hull, and the quarter gallery, which was shot away. Captain Wheelright was the only person wounded on board. We shot away the Libertador's main top-gallant mast, unshipped one of her gun carriages, took a chip off the after part of the foremast, killed two men, and cut her sails and rigging severely. We were immediately boarded by capt Davis of the Libertador, who pledged his honor, and that of Commodore Lopez, who was then on board, that we should receive honorable treatment as prisoners of war, as officers and gentlemen, and as soon as an exchange could be effected, we should be sent home. The kind attention and courtesy we have received from Commodore Lopez, Captain Davis and officers has been truly great for which we tender them our sincere thanks, likewise Captain Thompson of the schooner of war Bravo has extended every civility and kindness. We leave this place tomorrow for Matamoras: what disposition will be made of us I know not.

Besides the officers and crew of our vessel, we had on board as passengers, the honorable Wm. H. Wharton, Mr. Levy, Surgeon T. N., captain Darocher, T. A.,[1] Mr. Thayer, of Boston, Mr. Wooster, English subject, George Etess, acting lieutenant T. N. and Mr. Henry Childs.

I remain very respectfully, your obedient servent,

J. W. Taylor, Lieut.

[P. S.] Our crew consisted of 31 men and boys, besides the officers; out of this number there were six seamen, the balance not knowing one part of the ship from the other, and it was with great difficulty that we obtained this crew while in New Orleans.

[1] Intended for N.

Tennison's Journal mentions one incident connected with the surrender, not referred to in the official account. He says that upon Davis's demand to surrender Taylor said to him: "Sir, I am your prisoner, but my sword you shall never receive," so he threw it overboard.[1]

The surrender took place within plain view of Velasco, and the whole town, including the secretary of the navy, S. Rhoads Fisher, turned out to see the struggle. Their criticism of the government, for not keeping its vessels well manned and provisioned to guard the Texas coast, instead of leaving them in New Orleans for months trying to get outfitted, was the spur which impelled Fisher to give the matter his entire attention, and to take passage on the *Invincible* a few weeks after this, in order to give the Mexicans battle. His efforts, and their results have been noticed in the history of these two vessels.

The *Independence* and the prisoners were carried to Brazos Santiago by the victorious vessels.[2] The Mexican papers state that the *Independence* was bravely defended before she was taken. Their notices of the capture include also the information that one of her guns was an eight pounder, lost by the Mexicans some time since at San Jacinto. It was considered by the Texans one of their chief trophies, and bore the initials of many of the principal ladies of Texas. The principal officers of the *Independence* received the kindest of treatment through the special orders of President Bustamente. For the first three months of their imprisonment the crew were treated rather harshly, but after that they had no complaints to make. For many favors the officers and crew felt especially grateful to the president, to Commodore Lopez, and to Captains Martínez, Davis, and Thomas Thompson. Through the instrumentality of Captain Thompson, Captain Wheelwright and Dr. Levy, with the consent of all the officers of the *Independence,* made their escape early in July,[3] Captain Thompson accompanying them, and leaving the Mexican service to join the Texas navy.[4] After arriving in Texas, Thompson was

---

[1] Tennison's Journal, folio 316, p. 3.

[2] *Gazeta de Tampico*, April 29, 1837; *Mercurio de Matamoros*, April 21, 1837.

[3] New Orleans *Commercial Bulletin*, July 12, 1837.

[4] See *Telegraph and Texas Register*, July 8, 1837.

The Navy of the Republic of Texas. 65

appointed post-captain at Galveston, where Alex. Thompson, the chief hydrographer for Texas, had selected a suitable site for a navy yard[1] for the Republic. The interest that the Texan Congress took in the release of the prisoners, and President Houston's attitude toward the effort have already been noticed.[2] In his message of November 21, 1837,[3] Houston recites the unsuccessful attempt of the government, through the agency of John A. Wharton, to secure an exchange; but consoles himself with the fact that some of the prisoners escaped and that President Bustamente set the others free in October. Before learning of their release, Congress, spurred on by Houston, passed a joint resolution authorizing reprisals upon Mexico; but this was withdrawn upon their arrival at Galveston, November 4.

On December 14, 1837, Congress appropriated $250,000 for back pay of officers, soldiers, and sailors, and a joint resolution of December 18 authorized the auditor to settle with Thomas Brennan, purser of the *Independence,* the claims of the officers and crew of that vessel.[4]

There was one other vessel connected with the Texan naval establishment. Her mission seems to have been a peaceful one. This was the receiving vessel *Potomac.* She was purchased from Captain L. M. Hitchcock,[5] formerly a lieutenant on the *Invincible,* for $8000. Later, by recommendation of the secretary of the navy, she became a pilot boat at Galveston.

Here ends the history of the first navy of Texas. As early as 1836, however, the Republic of Texas was anxious to have a stronger navy, and Congress passed favorably on measures for procuring a new and stronger fleet, composed principally of steam vessels. The account of this movement, the acquisition of the vessels, and their history, is distinctly separate from that of the first navy of the Republic, and it will be given next.

[1]Burnet issued a decree on April 21, 1836, establishing a naval depot at Galveston Island. See *Texas Almanac,* 1869, p. 57.
[2]See pp, 263-264, above.
[3]*Telegraph and Texas Register,* November 25, 1837.
[4]Gammel, *Laws of Texas,* I, 1398, 1399.
[5]See *House Journal,* 3d Tex. Cong., 18.

IX. MEASURES TO PROCURE A SECOND NAVY.

The vessels of the first navy were lost through captures, wrecks, and other misfortunes. But Texas, possessing as she did such an extensive sea-board, could not expect to be regarded as a nation unless she had a navy strong enough to protect her coast and harbors. Emigrants would hesitate to risk their all in a voyage to a country not prepared to protect them if attacked *en route*. Trading vessels would be slow to bring those commodities to her shores which would be necessary for the comfort of the people. Exportation would likewise be dangerous. Shipowners would dread capture and loss of their vessels, with possible imprisonment in a Mexican dungeon. Excessive insurance would raise the price of all commodities to the point where the bare necessities of life would become luxuries. But, with proper protection, immigration would soon fill up the land; and the increased imports and exports, as the country became settled, would bring a revenue in the way of customs duties that would eventually pay for the maintenance of a navy. These considerations alone would justify the expenditure of a considerable sum by Texas; and when, in addition, it is remembered that Mexico had in no wise relinquished her intention of reconquering Texas, and would sooner or later attack her by land and by sea, the reader can understand why it was necessary for Texas to secure and maintain at any cost a navy strong enough to make Mexico fear and respect her, and to impress foreign nations with the stability of her government.

All this had been clearly perceived since the first session of the first congress of the Republic. On October 26, 1836, the Committee on Naval Affairs recommended "the immediate building or purchase" of one twenty-four gun sloop, a ten gun steam vessel, and two schooners of eleven guns each. The total cost of the four vessels was to be $135,000.[1] An act was passed in conformity with these resolutions, authorizing the President to appoint an agent to proceed immediately to the United States, to purchase, or contract for and superintend the building of, the desired vessels. It was approved by President Houston November 18, 1836. This increase in the navy was planned while Texas was still in pos-

---

[1] *House Journal*, 1st Tex. Cong., 1st Sess., 97-98; Gammel, *Laws of Texas*, I, 1090; Gouge, *Fiscal History of Texas*, 54.

session of several war vessels; but long before any of the vessels of the new navy reached the Texan shores, the last of the old navy, excepting the *Potomac,* had disappeared. Owing to the youth of the Republic, and the uncertainty of her future, sufficient money could not be borrowed to carry out the act; and it therefore remained ineffective.

The second congress found it imperative to act. The *Independence* had been captured by the Mexicans, and the *Invincible* wrecked, leaving the *Brutus* and the *Potomac* sole defenders of six hundred miles of coast. William M. Shepherd, acting secretary of the navy, in his report of September 30, 1837,[1] begs earnestly for the expenditure of a few thousand dollars to prevent Mexico's gaining supremacy of the Gulf. Some two weeks later the *Brutus* was wrecked, and the Committee on Naval Affairs thereupon framed the following resolutions, and submitted them to the Senate for action:[2]

Resolved that the Senate and the house of representatives of the Republic of Texas in congress assembled proceed to Elect by joint ballot an agent whose duty it shall be to repair immediately to Baltimore or some other seaport town of the United States of the north for the purpose of buying or building arming and equipping for the public service of the Republic of Texas one corvette of 18.24 medium, 2-10 Gun Briggs mounting medium 18 pounders—and two substantial schooners . . . provided the cost of said vessels shall not exceed $250,000 which said amount is hereby appropriated out of any unappropriated money now in, or that hereafter may be in the treasury. . . .

The resolution was amended to authorize the purchase of a five hundred ton ship mounting eighteen guns, two three hundred ton brigs of twelve guns each, and three schooners of one hundred and thirty tons, mounting five or seven guns each; to appropriate two hundred and eighty thousand dollars for the purpose; to instruct the secretary of the treasury to furnish said agent with a draft for the above appropriated sum on Messrs. Gilmer and Burnley, the "commissioners to negotiate a five million loan";[3] and to pledge solemnly the public faith for the payment of this

[1]*House Journal.* 2nd Texas Cong., 1st and 2nd Sessions, 166-172.
[2]Archives of the Department of State, file No. 764.
[3]Gammel, *Laws of Texas,* IX, 1355-1356.

amount. It became a law with the President's approval on November 4, 1837.[1]

To carry out the provisions of this act, President Houston appointed Peter W. Grayson agent. Grayson had represented Texas as commissioner to the United States in 1836, when the country was seeking recognition, and his appointment for the present task was considered a wise one. At about this time, however, he became candidate for the presidency of Texas, and during the campaign committed suicide in a fit of despondency at Bean's Station, Tennessee. John A. Wharton was anxious to succeed him, but President Houston appointed Samuel M. Williams.[2] Williams at once executed his bond, and departed for Baltimore, to enter actively into the labors of procuring a navy for Texas.

In order to meet immediate needs, an effort was made to buy the steam ship Pulaski; and Congress authorized her purchase at an agreed price;[3] but the transaction failed through the refusal of the owners to deliver her at Galveston, on the ground that our ports were declared by the enemy to be under blockade, and that the blockade was reported to be effective. Before any agreement could be arrived at she was destroyed. The *Potomac,* therefore, was the only vessel that was in the service of Texas during 1838. And for a long time it remained doubtful whether or not the government would become the owner of this vessel. The secretary of the navy at a critical hour had bought it on his own responsibility from Captain L. M. Hitchcock for eight thousand dollars and had almost completed its conversion into a brig of war, when all further work on it was suspended

[1] Gammel, *Laws of Texas,* I, 1355-1356; Gouge, *Fiscal History of Texas.* 70.

[2] Report of Secretary of Navy in *House Journal,* 3d Tex. Cong., 1st Sess., 15-20. The following amusing reason is given for the president's refusal to appoint John A. Wharton. He had previously appointed William H. Wharton minister to the United States to secure the recognition of Texan independence. It is related that Wharton was not pleased with the appointment, and remarked that the president was sending him into honorable exile to get him out of some one else's way. Houston did not hear of this until some months later, when John A. Wharton applied for the agency. Meeting William H. Wharton after his return from the United States, the president could not refrain from delivering a home thrust. "I did not appoint John A. Wharton naval commissioner," he said, "because I did not wish to drive any more of the Wharton family into exile."—Linn, *Reminiscences of Fifty Years in Texas,* 273.

[3] Gammel, *Laws of Texas,* I. 1392.

because congress had made no provision for its purchase. This, however, was due to a want of funds, and not to a belief in congress that the vessel was not needed. The secretary of the navy in his report of October 30, 1838, put the matter before the president, and urged him to find some means for completing the transaction.[1] The *Potomac* seems to have been finally acquired by the government, though no record of the transfer can be found. The secretary of the navy two years later says:[2]

In consequence of the leaky condition of the brig Potomac, formerly the receiving ship, she has had everything removed from her; placed securely in the yard, and her crew transferred to the Wharton. It has since been discovered, and prevented as far as it was deemed necessary, to keep her from sinking. This vessel is new and has been for a long while, perfectly useless to the Government for any purpose whatever, and, as an application has been made by the Commander of the station to transfer her to the pilot of Galveston, with a view of making a light boat of her, upon such terms as he believes would be beneficial to the public interest, I advise this measure, believing it will not interfere with the best interests of the navy, and that it will be of great advantage to our growing commerce.

Not another word we can find concerning her, except in the Tennison Papers, in the original order of A. C. Hinton commanding the naval station at Galveston, and addressed to William A. Tennison, midshipman, on board the *Potomac* at Galveston, ordering him to report to Lieutenant William S. Williamson on board the brig of war *Brazos,* for duty.[3] This is the only time the brig of war *Brazos* is mentioned officially or otherwise. Where she came from, or what became of her, no existing documents relate. Under another name, she may have played some part in Texas history. That there was such a vessel in the navy in 1842, there is no question, as the document mentioning it is original and genuine.

For the sake of economy, the president ordered the secretary of the navy to disband the officers and men of the navy until vessels could be procured for them. Only enough were retained to

---

[1] *House Journal*, 3d Tex. Cong., 18; Yoakum, II, 242.
[2] Report of November 4, 1840, in *House Journal*, 5th Tex. Cong., 1st Sess., Appendix, 185-196.
[3] Hinton to Tennison, an undated autograph letter signed.

man the *Potomac* and the naval station at Galveston.[1] This act, while a hardship on the officers and men, was proper under the circumstances, and proved quite a saving to the government; as it was some time before the men were needed.

Fate was very kind to Texas at this time, when she had no navy and was seemingly at the mercy of her enemy. The French government, having certain claims against Mexico, which Mexico declined to satisfy, assembled a considerable naval force at Vera Cruz and declared the Mexican ports blockaded. Shortly after the inauguration of the new president of Texas, M. B. Lamar, on December 9, 1838, Texas was gratified with the intelligence of the capture of Vera Cruz. The blockade of the French having failed to bring the government to terms, Admiral Baudin despatched a messenger to General Rincón, the Mexican commandant, informing him that he was about to attack the castle of San Juan d'Ulloa. This fortress, situated on an island in the harbor of Vera Cruz, was defended by one hundred and sixty pieces of artillery and some five thousand men. The bombardment commenced about two o'clock, in the afternoon of the 27th of November, and was so well directed that in four hours, after a loss of six hundred men in killed and wounded, the Mexicans capitulated and marched out of the castle, and the French took possession. The Mexican government thereupon despatched Santa Anna with five thousand men to drive the French out of the place. In attempting this, he lost his leg, and many of his troops were killed and wounded. On March 9, 1839, a treaty was made between Mexico and France, which was shortly afterwards ratified, and the French forces left the territory of the Republic.[2]

On his way home Admiral Baudin, with a part of the fleet, visited Texas. He was given a grand welcome to Galveston and to Texas. The mayor and aldermen of Galveston delivered the keys of the city to him, and Admiral Baudin, in a written response, declared that he was glad to have contributed by his work in Mexico to such a cause as the independence of the Texian nation. He said

[1] Report of Secretary of Navy, October 30, 1838, in *House Journal*, 3d Tex. Cong., 1st Sess., 15-16.
[2] Yoakum, II, 242, 253, 255.

. . . . I hope it will prove, too, beneficial to the several nations, who, either as friends or as foes, have to deal with Mexico. Nothing could be more gratifying to my feelings than to be considered as one of you, gentlemen, whose industry and energy I do so much admire. Be assured that I would vastly prefer being the humblest member of a well regulated and thriving community, like yours, than to moving in the sphere of wealth and power in a corrupt and decaying society. With the highest regard and respect, I have the honor to be, Gentlemen,

Your affectionate and devoted Serv't, CHARLES BAUDIN.[1]

To understand fully the gratitude of the people we must remember that, but for the opportune interference of the French, the whole coast of Texas would have been at the mercy of any fleet, however small, that Mexico might have sent against it. Can it be wondered at that Galveston and all Texas felt that France had helped to fight the battles of the Republic?

While Texas was thus enjoying a respite through the involuntary assistance of France, Mr. Williams, in Baltimore, was doing all in his power to obtain proper vessels for the navy. Owing to the fact that the loan was not effected with which to purchase the fleet, he was much discouraged. On October 9, 1838, he wrote from Philadelphia,[2] that the only prospect at that time was to buy the steam packet *Charleston*, which had been built eighteen months before at a cost of $117,000. She could be had for $120,000, payable in five years with ten per cent interest, and could be so altered as to make her an available naval ship. On November 3, 1848, General Hamilton, who was the regularly appointed consul for the Republic of Texas, in Charleston, addressed a lengthy communication to the secretary of the navy,[3] in regard to the purchase of this vessel. He said that while in England he had had the good fortune to induce his friend James Holford, Esq., of London, to advance the money necessary for her purchase and outfit; but Hamilton said:

As Mr. Holford is not a citizen, the title had to be taken for the boat in my name, and so it will continue until she gets out

---

[1] Baudin to Mayor and Aldermen of Galveston, May 13, 1839, in an unidentified newspaper clipping.
[2] *House Journal*, 5th Tex. Cong., 1st Sess., Appendix, 212.
[3] *Ibid.*, 214-216.

to Texas, and a regular transfer is made of her to your Government. . . . As Mr. Holford has acted with the utmost liberality and confidence, I trust your Government will have passed, in *secret session* forthwith, a resolution confirming Messrs. Burnley and Williams' contract with me, as the agent of this gentleman.[1]

Agreeable to this request, an act was passed sanctioning the contract for the *Charleston,* afterwards known as the *Zavala,* for the price of $120,000.[2] This vessel was, therefore, the first one of the new navy. Its final cost, as later altered and equipped, was much beyond the original contract price. But in this, as in other matters, the financial records of the navy are so tangled and obscure as to render details impossible. It would be alike tedious and unprofitable to attempt to unravel them. Indeed, the secretary of the navy, in 1840, confessed the task too heavy for himself[3]

Soon after the *Zavala* had been arranged for, Mr. Williams was successful in concluding a contract, on November 13, 1838, with Frederick Dawson, of Baltimore, for one ship, two brigs, and three schooners to be fully armed, furnished with provisions and munitions, and delivered in the port of Galveston.[4] For this it was agreed that,

the bonds of the Government of Texas, made and executed by the Commissioners for the Loan, shall be executed and signed and deposited in the Bank of the United States of Pennsylvania, or the Girard Bank at Philadelphia, . . . for five hundred and sixty thousand dollars, there to remain . . . as security . . . for the space of twelve calendar months, which bonds are to bear . . . a rate of interest of ten per cent per annum, . . . which bonds can be redeemed at the end of twelve months,

---

[1]Hamilton to Secretary of Navy, November 3, 1838, in *House Journal,* 5th Tex. Cong., 1st Sess., Appendix, 214-216.

[2]Gouge, *Fiscal History of Texas,* 93.

[3]Secretary of the Navy, Report of November 4, 1840, in *House Journal,* 5th Tex. Cong., 1st Sess., Appendix, 187; see also Gouge, *Fiscal History of Texas,* 93, 94, 198-199, 206, 305.

[4]For the contract with Dawson see *House Journal,* 5th Tex. Cong., 1st Sess., Appendix, 202-204. See also Yoakum, II, 243; Gouge, *Fiscal History of Texas,* 94; and Report of Special Committee to the Senate, January 22, 1854. Dawson turned his interest over to S. Chott and Whitney; these two gentlemen, in a lengthy letter addressed to the government of Texas, October 9, 1851, complained bitterly of the effort made to scale the bonds, and their arguments seem unanswerable. See Gouge, *Fiscal History of Texas,* 198-199.

The Navy of the Republic of Texas. 73

by the payment of the two hundred and eighty thousand dollars, and the ten per cent which shall have accrued . . . in Gold or Silver. . . . If the Government of Texas shall prefer to instruct the Loan Commissioners to issue, or shall itself issue sterling bonds for the sum of five hundred and twenty thousand dollars at any time prior to the first day of February next, he will receive them in full liquidation, and payment of the debt hereby contracted, and in lieu of the bonds heretofore mentioned.

On receiving the intelligence that the navy had been contracted for, the Texas government, on January 26, passed an act which declared that, whereas the agent of the Republic had made a contract for the purchase of one ship of eighteen guns, two brigs of twelve guns each, and three schooners of six guns each, and,

whereas it has become indispensably necessary, in order to prepare and keep in service the said vessels, as well for the protection of the coasts and harbors of Texas, as for the protection of the commerce thereof, that an appropriation be made of the sum required for that object. Wherefore, be it enacted, . . . That the sum of two hundred and fifty thousand dollars, in the promissory notes of the Government be, and the sum is hereby appropriated for the naval service for the year 1839. . . .[1]

The navy thus contracted for, including the *Zavala*, and the appropriation just mentioned, cost the Texan government more than $800,000.[2]

Mr. Williams, having now accomplished the task he had been entrusted with, returned to Texas. That his services were appreciated by his countrymen, we note in a resolution offered in congress[3] tendering him a resolution of thanks "for the energy which he has rendered in procuring a navy." It will be recalled that while he was connected with the firm of McKinney and Williams he had been largely instrumental in securing the first navy of Texas. His talent lay in his ability to finance such matters, and later in life we see him the first banker of Texas. He knew noth-

---

[1]Gammel, *Laws of Texas*, II, 129-130. Gouge, *Fiscal History of Texas*, 93, and Bancroft, II, 317, say that this appropriation of $250,000 was made to pay for the ships contracted for; they are of course, mistaken, as the language of the act is clear.

[2]Secretary of the navy, Report of November 8, 1839, cited in Yoakum, II, 272; Bancroft, II, 351.

[3]*Senate Journal*, 3d Tex. Cong., 1st Sess., 72. The resolution was dated December 14, 1838.

ing of naval construction, and the republic now needed a man at Baltimore to see that the contract was carried out according to specifications. A man in every respect qualified for this important service was found in John G. Tod, who had resigned a commission in the United States navy to connect himself with the young republic.[1] Before entering upon the work, he had, at the request of the secretary of the navy, drawn up a report upon the establishment of a navy yard, and in April, 1838, had been vested with powers to examine into and report on all matters connected with the naval interests. On June 10, 1838, he was ordered to the United States by President Houston upon that mission. He fitted out the steamer *Charleston* and returned with her to Galveston, in March, 1839, where her name and flag were changed, and she

---

[1] John G. Tod was born in Kentucky. Leaving Lexington when seventeen years of age, he proceeded down the Mississippi on a flatboat to New Orleans, and enlisted in the Mexican Navy as a midshipman, under Admiral Mina. Two years later, through the influence of Henry Clay, he was appointed a midshipman in the United States navy, and transferred to that service in which he rose to more important grades.—C. W. Raines, *Year Book of Texas*, 1901, p. 402.

Mr. Tod entered the Texas navy in 1837, and, as the following letter (copied from a facsimile of the original) indicates, apparently had some difficulty in convincing the secretary of the navy of his merits:

Houston, May 25, 1837.

Hon. W. G. Hill.

Sir,—I take the liberty of laying the enclosed letters before you as a further introduction to your friendly enfluence in my behalf.

They will show you how I stand in civil life with men of eminence in the United States—who are not likely to confer their friendship or esteem upon any man except for his individual worth as a gentleman; more especially, when the difference of *rank* betwen us as public men is taken into consideration.

The Hon. James Harlan is from Kentucky and has known me from my earliest years. Commodores Barron and Bolton are at the head of the Navy. Maj. Graham is a distinguished officer of the U. S. Army. The first clause of his letter will inform you how I stand with my acquaintances in the U. S. Navy.

I regret that the present state of affairs should make it necessary for me (to succeed in my object) to trouble you and other gentlemen upon a subject that the Hon. Secretary of the Navy alone appears to view in rather an indifferent light. If I obtain my commission, it will be my pride to do my duty in every situation that my country places me. My greatest honor to prove myself worthy of the interest shown by my friends. My glory in defending the rights and advancing the liberties of our common country.

Very respectfully,

I have the honor to be, Sir, your ob. Servt,

JNO. G. TOD

was commissioned as the *Zavala*.[1] In accordance with the Dawson contract, on June 27, 1839, the schooner *San Jacinto* was delivered; on August 7, the schooner *San Antonio;* on August 31, the schooner *San Bernard;* and, on October 18, the brig *Colorado*.[2] A corvette and a brig were yet wanting to complete the contract, but they were confidently expected by the end of the year.[3] They were in fact delivered, one in January, and the other in April, 1840. The following account appeared in a current newspaper:[4]

Texian Navy.—The following list of vessels constitute the present naval force of Texas. As there are a number of officers of that service who were officers of our navy, these details may be interesting to many of the readers of the *Chronicle*.

Steamer Zavalla—An efficient and well appointed vessel.

Sloop Trinity—600 tons, carries 20 24 pounders, medium guns.

Brigs { Colorado, Galveston } 400 tons, carries each 16 18 pounder medium guns.

Schooners { San Jacinto, San Bernard, San Antone } 170 tons, each carrying 7 12 pounders, and 1 long eighteen, on a pivot.

Brig Potomac—Receiving vessel.

These vessels, with the exception of the steamer and receiving vessel, were built, equipped, and provisioned under the immediate superintendence of John G. Tod, Esq., Texan Naval Agent of the United States, a gentleman well and favorably known in this country, having at an early period in his life held an honorable place in our navy.

The secretary of the navy in his report[5] of 1840 said:

. . . Mr. Dawson has delivered the brig and the sloop-of-war then due; and everything else appertaining to this contract has been complied with in the most generous and liberal manner. The brig and sloop-of-war, like all the other vessels, have been constructed on a much more commodious scale than the contract re-

---

[1]As an instance of the carelessness of the historians of Texas it may be mentioned that Yoakum (II, 271), Morphis (419), and Brown (II, 128), each represents the *Charleston* and the *Zavala* as two separate vessels. That such an error should have been made by Yoakum, who used the documents, is strange; Morphis and Brown, no doubt, followed Yoakum's statement without consulting the sources.

[2]In 1840 the name of the *Colorado* was changed to the *Archer*.

[3]Secretary of the navy, Report of November 8, 1839; Yoakum, II, 271.

[4]An unidentified newspaper clipping, containing matter copied from an issue of the *Army and Navy Chronicle* of date not indicated.

[5]In *House Journal*, 5th Tex. Cong., 1st Sess., Appendix, 185-196.

quired, and have been furnished in a more suitable manner than that for which the contractors were obligated. The brig, which was the last vessel received on the contract, was delivered at Galveston with the naval equipments belonging to her, and the other vessels, on the 25th April 1840,[1]—the ship on the 5th January previous. . . .

This officer[2] is entitled to great credit for the management and system shown in his operations. His attention to the complicated duties entrusted to him in the United States, as well as his conduct in direct connection with this Department, has always been faithful and laborious, and meets my cordial approbation.

Captain Tod wrote a very appreciative letter of thanks to Dawson,[2] which received a suitable reply. Captain Tod said in part:

The last vessel included in the contract entered into by yourself on one part, and the Republic of Texas of the other part, having received from me the certificate approving of the same, I feel it a duty as well as a pleasure to express to you the satisfaction I have in testifying to the very creditable and liberal manner in which the contract has been fulfilled on your part.

I will not indulge in any useless expressions of my opinion of these vessels, they speak for themselves, and many persons of acknowledged judgment in naval architecture, have pronounced them equal to any that have ever sailed from this port, in beauty of model, strength and duribility of materials and finished specimens of workmanship. . . .

John G. Tod,
Naval Agent of Texas to the U. S.

On the return of Captain Tod to Galveston, June 3, 1840, he was invited to partake of a public dinner tendered him by the citizens of Galveston at the Tremont House. The committee on invitation were M. B. Menard, P. J. Menard, James Love, Levi Jones, and Thomas F. McKinney. From this he excused himself on the plea of pressing business, but thanked them for their appreciation of his services, declaring that,

The greatest happiness a public servant has in this life, is the satisfaction of feeling that he has been faithful and conscientious in the discharge of such duties as may have been entrusted to him.

[1]These two vessels were the *Austin* and the *Wharton*. The latter had formerly been the *Dolphin*.
[2]Captain John G. Tod.
[3]Tod to Dawson, March 19, 1840, in *House Journal*, 5th Tex. Cong., 1st Sess., Appendix, 199.

The Navy of the Republic of Texas.

If this pleasure can be enhanced, it is by the assurance that his humble efforts in behalf of his country's interest meet the approbation of his fellow citizens.[1]

Captain Tod's last letter as naval agent, among other matters, highly compliments "H. H. Williams, our consul in Baltimore, to whom was entrusted the purchase of our supplies under my direction," and acknowledges at the same time his indebtedness to Commodores Barron and Warrington, of the United States navy, and to Francis Grice, naval constructor of the Norfolk dockyards, "for much useful information imparted to me by these gentlemen."[2]

On June 24, 1840, Captain Tod was placed in command of the naval station at Galveston.

X. EARLY TROUBLES OF THE NEW NAVY.

By the end of April, 1840, the make-up of the second navy was completed. It consisted of the *Potomac, Zavala, Austin, Wharton, Archer, San Bernard, San Jacinto,* and *San Antonio.* The *Zavala,* formerly the *Charleston,* was named for Lorenzo de Zavala; the *Austin,* for Stephen F. Austin; the *Wharton,* formerly the *Dolphin,* for the Wharton brothers,—William H. and John A.;—and the *Archer,* formerly the *Colorado,* for Dr. Branch T. Archer. Besides these vessels references are found to the *Trinity,*[3] the *Galveston,*[4] the *Houston,*[5] the *Merchant,*[6] the *Texas,*[7] the *Asp,*[8] and the *Brazos.* The first two were apparently a part of the Dawson contract, and doubtless became incorporated in the fleet under changed names; the *Houston* seems to have been a Yucatán auxiliary, temporarily

[1]Tod to Galveston Gentlemen, Juen 4, 1840, in Tennison's Journal.
[2]*House Journal*, 5th Tex. Cong., 1st Sess., Appendix, 198.
[3]An unidentified newspaper clipping, with matter copied from an issue of the *Army and Navy Chronicle* of date not indicated.
[4]*Ibid.*
[5]Jones, *Republic of Texas*, 194.
[6]Moore, *To the People of Texas*, 86.
[7]Journal of Midshipman James L. Mabry in *Galveston News*, January 9, 16, 23, 1893. This Journal, together with the Ledger and Ration Book of the Texas Navy are the property of Mrs. R. W. Shaw, of Galveston, daughter of Captain James G. Hurd, formerly first lieutenant of the *Brutus*, and granddaughter of Captain Norman Hurd, purser in the Texas navy.
[8]*Ibid.*

acting with the Texans; and the *Merchant* was the private property of E. W. Moore. Of the other vessels mentioned nothing further is known.

This brings us to the *personnel* of the new navy, and we will now introduce the officers, renewing old acquaintances and forming new ones. The man that stands out pre-eminently for his individuality, as well as high position in the navy, is Commodore Edwin Ward Moore. Born in June, 1810, at Alexandria, Virginia, where he received his education, he entered the United States navy as a midshipman, at the age of fourteen, and remained in the service for nearly fifteen years.[1] In a letter written in 1904, George F. Fuller, one of his midshipmen in the Texas navy, speaks of him as about 5 feet 8 inches in height, of fair complexion, blue eyes, light brown hair, and stocky build. He was genial, pleasant, and universally liked; a thorough seaman and a splendid officer.[2] In 1839 the prospect of an adventurous and active career in the Texas navy caused him to resign his commission as lieutenant on the United States sloop *Boston*,[3] and offer his services to Texas. He was appointed post-captain and was generally addressed by the title of Commodore, both by the public and by the secretary of the navy in his official communications. He had command of the entire Texas navy from the beginning of his service. Strange, however, as it may seem, no commission was issued to him, or the officers under him, until three years after they had entered the Texan service. In a letter to the secretary of war and marine July 5, 1842, he complained of this in the following terms:

> I beg leave also to call the attention of the Department to the fact that *not an officer in the Navy has a commission*, a circumstance unprecedented in the annals of history, that a Government should have for three years, their vessels of war on the high seas, visiting foreign ports, and capturing the enemy's vessels, without a commission even in the possession of the commander of the Navy.[4]

This letter seems to have had the effect that Commodore Moore desired, for two weeks later he received his commission, as did

---

[1]Till July 16, 1839. *Cong. Globe*, 33d Cong., 1st Sess., Appendix, 1084; Moore, *To the People of Texas*, 10.

[2]Fuller to Dienst, October 27, 1904, in Dienst Col. Docs.

[3]Thrall, 592.

[4]Moore to Hockley, in Moore's *To the People of Texas*, 79.

also the officers serving under him. These commissions were confirmed by the senate on July 20, 1842. Commodore Moore's commission entitled him, "Post Captain Commanding," and was antedated April 21, 1839, some time before his resignation from the United States navy.

The first difficulty encountered by the new navy was to obtain sufficient sailors and marines to man the ships.[1] For this purpose the *San Antonio* was, in November, 1839, at New Orleans, on recruiting service.[2] At the same time the secretary of the navy ordered the *Zavala* to New Orleans for refitting. Captain A. C. Hinton of the *Zavala* was instructed not to allow his expenditure to exceed $9000, including $3200 for the enlistment of sailors and marines.[3] He went, however, considerably beyond the modest limit set by the department, incurred a severe reprimand therefor from the secretary, and was ordered to return to Galveston. The reproof administered to him was in part as follows:

You appear to have forgotten the very first principle of naval discipline, to wit: that *the first duty of an officer, as well as a seaman, consists in obeying orders.* If you have so far transcended yours, as to purchase *anything* for which you can not show definite orders, be assured that you will be held responsible; and you furthermore are strictly forbidden from incurring, under any pretext whatever, any liabilities against the Government for repairs. . . . You will . . . return as soon as possible to Galveston, and report immediately to this Department.[4]

In reporting the matter to President Lamar the secretary used a different tone. He said that, though Hinton had exceeeded his allowance by nearly twelve thousand dollars, yet

on the return of the Zavala to Galveston, her natural efficiency was found to be very much increased, and I have no hesitation in

---

[1] In regard to the proceedings of the United States government against Moore himself on the charge of illegal recruiting activity in New York Harbor in the winter of 1839-40, see Deposition of Hunter. December 30, 1839; Forsyth to Dunlap, January 15, 1840; Dunlap to Forsyth, January 16, 1840—all in Annual Report American Historical Association for 1907, Volume II.—EDITOR QUARTERLY.

[2] Moore to Hinton, *House Journal*, 5th Tex. Cong., 1st. Sess., Appendix, 223-224.

[3] *House Journal*, 5th Tex. Cong., 1st Sess., Appendix, 221-222.

[4] Cooke to Hinton, December 21, 1839, in *House Journal*, 5th Tex. Cong., 1st Sess., Appendix, 238-239.

saying, that the unauthorized repairs were essentially needed, and they would have been suggested by the proper authority, except for the consciousness of inability to pay for them.[1]

The President considered the breach of discipline as serious enough to warrant the withdrawal of Hinton's commission. Hinton appealed to congress, and a joint resolution was passed,[2] ordering the secretary of the navy to organize a court-martial for the trial of Hinton, and declaring that in future no officer should be deprived of his commission except by sentence of such a court. The verdict of the court-martial was favorable to Hinton, and congress passed another joint resolution acquitting him "of any act of misconduct reflecting upon him as an officer or gentleman whilst a commander in the Navy of this Republic."[3]

The *Zavala*, on her return to Galveston, had brought a considerable number of men to complete the equipment of the other vessels. For a while it seemed as if this act, and all the cost of provisioning and officering the new navy were to be in vain. The lawmakers of Texas, in the mood of retrenching and economizing, were about to sacrifice an outlay of one million dollars, in order to save a few thousands. Without warning, or ascribing any cause for its action, congress passed a law which was approved on February 5, 1840, requiring the president to retire from the service temporarily all the fleet except such schooners as were needed for revenue purposes, and to retain only a sufficient number of officers and men to carry out the provisions of the act. Section 4, however, provided that, "should Mexico make any hostile demonstrations upon the Gulf, the President may order any number of vessels into active service, that he may deem necessary for the public security."[4]

That the President was not in sympathy with this act can be clearly seen in reading his message of November, 1840. He probably acquiesced in it with the intention of availing himself of the discretionary power conferred by Section 4. At any rate, he did

---

[1]Secretary of the navy, Report of November 4, 1840, *House Journal*, 5th Tex. Cong., 1st Sess., Appendix, 185-196.

[2]Gammel, *Laws of Texas*, II, 609.

[3]The resolution was approved January 29, 1842. It does not appear in Gammel's *Laws*, but the enrolled copy of the original may be found in the Records of the State Department (Texas).

[4]Gammel, *Laws of Texas*, II, 364.

not execute the act, and concerning his reasons for not doing so, spoke as follows:[1]

The act of the last session of congress providing for the laying up in ordinary the principal portion of the naval forces of the country, has not been carried into effect. Before the necessary preparations could be made for doing so, circumstances transpired, which in the opinion of the executive, involved potentially the contingency contemplated in the fourth section of that act, and induced him to defer the withdrawal of our gallant flag from the gulf. It was confidently asserted in the papers of the United States, and as confidently believed here, that the Mexican government had made a contract in Europe for the purchase of several vessels of war, and that she had actually procured an armed steam ship from a commercial house in England, with a view of making a descent upon the coast of Texas, and of cutting off our commerce with foreign nations; and during the prevalence of that opinion, the executive would have been violating the evident intention and spirit of the act of congress, instead of carrying it into effect, had he caused the seamen already in the service to be disbanded, and the vessels to be laid up in ordinary. Other events, also, occurred about the same time, and conspired with these considerations to dissuade me from dismantling a navy which had been equipped at a great expense, and which was manned and officered in a style of gallantry and efficiency inferior to none other of similar magnitude. Yucatan and Tabasco, lately forming a part of the confederate states of Mexico, wearied of the oppressions that followed the overthrow of the federal system in that republic, seceded from the central government, and uniting together pronounced their determination to be free. Similarity of circumstances and design naturally creates a sympathy of feeling, and would prompt this government to regard with peculiar interest the efforts of the citizens of the southern provinces to do precisely what we had so recently accomplished. But considerations of a higher character suggested the propriety of making a demonstration of our naval power on the coast of the new republic. It was expected to ascertain from the authorities established there in what relation this government should regard them, and whether their secession from Mexico would terminate their belligerent condition towards Texas. . . . It was considered advisable to communicate to the authorities our friendly dispositions, and to convey them with such a palpable exhibition of our power as would render them efficacious and permanent; and I am gratified to remark that these professions were readily and kindly received, and cordially reciprocated by the new government.

[1] See *House Journal*, 5th Tex. Cong., 1st Sess., 20-22.

Under these various circumstances, I have considered it my duty to keep the Navy at sea for a short period. But I was constrained by a sense of justice and regard to the sacred faith of the country to abstain from making captures of Mexican property, while our accredited agents were engaged in Mexico in a negotiation for peace with that Government. The naval equipments of a country, and especially of this country, are essentially different to the facility of organization from the military power. Competent officers and soldiers to constitute an army, may at any time be selected from the body of the population, but seamen and efficient naval officers are not to be found among a rural people, they belong to the element on which they serve, and are nurtured only on the ocean waves. To have disbanded the accomplished and gallant officers who have embarked in our naval service, at the moment when we had reason to believe our enemy was preparing a naval armament for our coast, would, in the opinion of the executive, have not only been indiscreet and impolitic, but would, as he believes, have been contrary to the true intention and meaning of congress, as expressed in the act of the last session. It is true it might have saved us some expenditure, but it is equally true, that it might have involved the country in great disaster, and an irreparable loss of reputation.

The information afforded by this message is sufficient warrant for its lengthy quotation. We see that the navy was not laid up in ordinary,[1] and that the officers and men were not disbanded. On the contrary, soon after the new fleet was ready for service it was permitted to have a trial.

XI. CRUISE OF THE TEXAS FLEET, 1840-1841.

In June the Texas fleet sailed for Mexico. For this movement quite a number of different causes have been alleged. According to President Lamar, the object of the expedition was to impress Yucatán with the strength of Texas, and thus establish diplomatic relations with this revolting state. According to Commodore Moore, it was the proclamation of the Mexican president, declaring Texan ports in a state of blockade. And, according to the secre-

[1] Eugene C. Barker, in *University of Texas Record*, V, 155, says: "Six months after Lamar assumed the reins of government the delivery of these naval vssels began, but the financial straits of the young republic made it necessary to place them temporarily in ordinary. For this needful act of economy he was blamed." That the vessels were not placed in ordinary this message shows; although, of course, the act approved by Lamar implied that it would be done.

The Navy of the Republic of Texas. 83

tary of the navy, it was because of a threatened invasion of Texas by Mexico, and the termination of the diplomatic mission of the agent of Texas, Mr. Treat. While it is peculiar to see these officials disagreeing as to the chief motive for such an expedition, it is most likely that all the causes they mention contributed to the movement For some seven months the naval establishment had been getting ready for such an expedition; and, while the act of congress had paralyzed the movement for a short time, it was only momentarily checked. With the consent and encouragement of President Lamar, the outfitting continued. The most formidable fleet Texas ever possessed left Galveston harbor on June 24, 1840, with Commodore E. W. Moore in command.

The fleet consisted of the *Austin,* carrying twenty guns, the flagship of Commodore Moore; the steamship *Zavala,* carrying eight guns; and the schooners, *San Bernard, San Jacinto,* and *San Antonio,* each carrying five guns.[1] The Brig *Wharton* commanded by

[1]The lists of officers of the various ships follow: the *Austin,* E. P. Kennedy, first lieutenant; D. H. Crisp, second lieutenant; J. H. Baker, third lieutenant; William Seegar, fourth lieutenant; C. Cummings, acting master; J. B. Gardiner, surgeon; Norman Hurd, purser; T. W. Sweet, lieutenant of marines; C. A. Christman, C. Leay, C. B. Snow, George F. Fuller, M. H. Dearborne, L. E. Bennett, J. C. Bronough, E. A. Wezman, W. W. McFarlane, R. H. Clements, midshipmen; John W. Brown, boatswain; John Salter, gunner; William Smith, carpenter; C. Cremer, sailmaker: the *Zavala,* J. T. K. Lothrop, captain; George Henderson, first lieutenant; W. C. Brashear, second lieutenant; Daniel Lloyd, master; T. P. Anderson, surgeon; W. T. Maury, purser; J. W. C. Parker, captain of marines; G. Beatty, chief engineer; R. Bache, captain's clerk; C. Betts, C. C. Cox, J. E. Barrow, H. (S). Garlick, J. A. Hartman, midshipmen; James Crout, boatswain; T. Howard, gunner; Joseph Auld, carpenter: the *San Bernard,* W. S. Williamson, lieutenant commanding; George W. Estes, first lieutenant; W. A. Tennison, second lieutenant (Ben C. Stuart, in *Galveston News,* October 8, 1899, has G. C. Bunner, second lieutenant, and W. A. Tennison, as acting master); Charles B. Snow, R. M. Clarke, surgeons; J. F. Stephens, purser; W. H. Brewster, captain's clerk; C. B. Underhill, John P. Stoneall, J. B. F. Bernard, L. H. Smith, midshipmen; George Brown, boatswain: the *San Jacinto,* W. R. Postell, lieutenant commanding; J. O. Shaughnessey, first lieutenant; A. G. Gray, second lieutenant; William Oliver, acting master; Fletcher Dorey, surgeon; Robert Oliver, purser; J. J. Tucker, captain's clerk; C. S. Arcamble, A. Walker, J. O. Parker, midshipmen: the *San Antonio,* Alex Moore, lieutenant commanding; Thomas Wood, Junior, first lieutenant; A. J. Lewis, second lieutenant; A. A. Waite, acting master; James W. Moore, purser; Hugh A. Goldborough, captain's clerk; James H. Wheeler, E. F. Wells, L. M. Minor, midshipmen; Hugh Schofield, boatswain.
The muster rolls here given are from the Tennison Papers (folio 352, pp. 1-3). They are the only complete rolls I have been able to secure. Yet Tennison's rolls cannot be depended upon as absolutely accurate. For other lists see Ben C. Stuart in *Galveston News,* October 8, 1899.

George Wheelwright, the *Archer* commanded by J. Clark, and the *Potomac* were left at Galveston. This was done, partly for the reason that they were not in condition to sail with the squadron, and partly because they were needed to protect Galveston in case Mexican vessels threatened the city or the coast.[1]

The itinerary and incidents of this cruise can be most briefly and clearly given by citing extracts of the report of Commodore E. W. Moore to the secretary of the navy:[2]

TEXAS SLOOP-OF-WAR AUSTIN,
At Sea, August 28th, 1840.
Latitude 25° 21' N.: Longitude 96° 29' W.

Sir: . . . 22d July . . . I order[ed] the Zavala to make the best of her way to the Arcos[3] Islands, touching at Sisal, under English colors, and to leave a letter for Gen. Anaya from Gen. Canales.[4] On the 26th July, the weather still very light, in consequence of which, and my unexpected detention off the S. W. Pass, I thought it best to send a vessel off Point Mariandrea with the letters No. 1 and 2 for Richard Packenham, Esq.,[5] her Britannic Majesty's Minister to Mexico; and that I might, in conformity of my orders of 20th June, endeavor to ascertain the feelings of the authorities of the State of Yucatan towards our Government,[6] and be off the Brazos de Santiago as near the time mentioned in the same orders as possible, I sent the schooner San Jacinto with

Alex Moore and James W. Moore, mentioned above, were a cousin and a brother of Commodore E. W. Moore. See Moore, *To the People of Texas*, 70-72, 110.

[1]The ships and officers mentioned in Brown's *History of Texas*, II, 198, footnote (copied in full without credit being given from *Texas Almanac*, 1860, pp. 165-166), have nothing whatever to do with this squadron, though, to the general reader, it would appear from the language used that they belonged to the Texas navy in 1840. Thrall, 306, note, says that the *Dolphin (Wharton)* sailed. There is, however, abundant evidence to the contrary.

[2]Moore to Cooke, *House Journal*, 5th Tex. Cong., 1st Sess., Appendix, 232-237. Moore's orders dated June 20, 1840, were sealed, and were to be opened at sea. On or about this date, the schooners *San Jacinto*, *San Antonio*, and *San Bernard*, sailed "for the west." The *Zavala* and the *Austin* were to have gone to sea on the 23d, but were detained by unfavorable weather. They sailed on June 27, 1840. See *Telegraph and Texas Register*, July 1, 1840.

[3]Arcas.

[4]Anaya and Canales were both leaders of the Mexican Federalists.

[5]Pakenham assisted Treat in presenting his proposition, and acted as mediator.—Bancroft, *History of Texas*, II, 340.

[6]This goes to show that president Lamar was correct in his statement of the object of the expedition.

the letters, and availing myself of the usual trade winds, proceeded with the San Bernard in company to Sisal, off which place I arrived on the 31st July, and, on making signal for a boat, wearing American colors, was boarded by an officer, and learned that the Zavala had passed six days before; he informed me that an order had been received that day from Merida (the Capitol,) by the captain of the Port, who had sent him out, that, if any Texian vessel appeared off the port, to offer her every facility,—upon which I hoisted our proper colors. . . . as soon as he left, filled away for Campeachy, where I was informed Gen. Anaya was. Arrived off Campeachy on the 2d August, and, while standing in under our own colors, we were met about eight miles from the land by a schooner of war, having on board Gen. Anaya and suite, who came on board.

On being informed by the General that he had not received the letter sent by the Zavala, and being no longer in doubt as to the disposition of the authorities, from their trusting a vessel of war, mounting *five* guns, along-side of this vessel and the San Bernard, and, knowing that the letter was of importance, as it had been written by Gen. Canales, after frequent interviews with his Excellency the President, I sent the San Bernard back to Sisal, with Gen. Anaya's secretary on board for it, and anchored. Gen. Anaya remained on board until after dark, and showed me letters from Galveston written sixteen or eighteen days before I left there . . . the next day . . . I had an interview with the Governor elect, Don Santiago Mendez. . . . He was anxious that the most friendly relations should be established at an early period, and assured me that the ports of the State of Yucatan were open to any Texian vessel. . . .

I left orders for the San Bernard to remain at Campeachy on her return from Sisal, until the 13th inst. . . .

On the 6th instant I received a letter from Gen. Anaya, . . . and the next day sailed for Point Mariandrea. On arriving off the Arcos[1] Islands on the 10th, I found the Zavala, . . .

I . . . the next day . . . sailed for Campeachy . . . where I arrived and anchored on the 13th inst., . . .

The naval force of the State of Yucatan consists of *one* small brig and *two* schooners. . . .

On the 14th the San Bernard arrived from Sisal, and the next morning we got under way; and the following morning, by 7 o'clock, were off the Arcos Islands; sent the San Barnard in to put Lieut. A. J. Lewis on board the Zavala, he having broken his leg some days previous by falling from the trunk of the schooner

[1] Arcas.

while giving an order and looking aloft, . . . and pushed on to meet the San Jacinto.

Arrived off point Mariandrea on the 18th; on the 19th, fell in with the San Bernard, and on the 20th, with the San Jacinto, when I was informed by Lieut. Postell that he had arrived off the point on the 1st inst. . . . . I have since met with . . . Her Britannic Majesty's brig Penguin, on her way from Vera Cruz to Tampico, and I was informed by her that it had been reported at Vera Cruz that there was a pirate off that part of the coast, and the brig was looking out for her. The officer appeared much pleased with the bold manner in which Lieut. Postell stood down for him, and I take this occasion to state to the Department that he is *much* the most efficient officer I have under my command.

. . .

On the 23d, not having fallen in with either the San Antonio or brig Wharton[1] which vessels I had ordered to meet me off Point Mariandrea, . . . I determined to stand down off Vera Cruz, under American colors, and board the first vessel that came out, in hopes of hearing whether Mr. Treat had left Mexico or not, and at the same time have a look at their shipping. That afternoon I was within three miles of the castle of Juan de Ulloa; stood off all night, and the next day, in the afternoon, an English brig came out; the wind being light, did not get near her until the next morning, when she sent her boat alongside with a letter from Mr. Treat, enclosing *one* to his Excellency the President, and *two* to the Hon. A. S. Lipscomb, Secretary of State.

The brig was Her Majesty's brig Penguin, and I learned from the officer who came on board from her, that the Centralists had no vessel of war at Vera Cruz; that the sloop-of-war *Iguala* was expected soon from France, that they were about purchasing a French ship there, lying in the harbor, and that the steamer Agyle was in the employment of the Mexican Government. . . .

. . . I thought it best to leave the San Bernard . . . Under the orders of which the enclosed is a copy; and in order that the letters which I had in my possession from the City of Mexico might reach their destination as early as possible, I made sail immediately, the San Jacinto in Company, for Galveston; and by the time we get in the latitude of the Brazos de Santiago, I will have finished my letters, when I will send the schooner on with them, and proceed myself to the Brazos, off which place I will not remain more than four days, (unless I meet additional orders

---

[1]The *Wharton*, by order of the secretary of the navy, was partly dismantled and placed in ordinary. This is the reason she did not at this time reach the squadron. See Secretary of the Navy, Report of November 4, 1840, in *House Journal*, 5th Tex. Cong., Appendix, 185-196.

from the Department,) when I will return with all dispatch off Point Mariandrea.

My not having fallen in with the San Antonio or brig Wharton has placed me in a disagreeable situation, as, from the force of circumstances, I can only appear off the Brazos with this vessel, when I am required by my orders, to appear off that place with the whole squadron; besides I am behind the time named, in consequence of waiting off Point Mariandrea, in the hope of meeting the San Antonio, at all events, as there was a probability of the Wharton not getting to sea.

. . . C. S. Nash, ordinary seaman, died on board this vessel on the 4th inst, while at Campeachy; his disease was dropsy, and he was transferred from the San Bernard on the 28th June, in order that he might be more comfortable. The San Jacinto also lost one man, who had been sick some time and was very old.

The Zavala has fully realized my expectations as a sea steamer. She left New-Orleans not quite *two-thirds* filled with coal, having about 1700 barrels on board; and she can carry 2700 barrels. The coal was of the most inferior kind, the blacksmith on board this vessel not being able to get a *welding heat on iron* with some of it we got from here. Filled with good Pittsburgh coal, a good head of steam can be kept up on her for thirty-five days; and, in the event of active operations on this coast, it will be necessary for her to have two thousand barrels of good Pittsburgh coal as soon as it can reach here, say about the 25th Sept., or 1st Oct., at which time she may be found at the Arcos Islands, the latitude of which is 20° 12′ N., and the latitude[1] 91° 57′ W. She adds greatly to the efficiency of our force, particularly on the coast of Mexico, where there is for so great a portion of the time very little wind, unless it is blowing a gale, which seldom lasts long.

. . .

I am, very respectfully,   Your obedient servent,
[Signed]   E. W. MOORE,
Captain Commanding.

To the Hon. Louis P. Cooke,
    Secretary of the Navy, Austin, Texas.

The following excerpts are taken from the diary of one of the midshipmen, and tell many events not mentioned by Commodore Moore in his dispatch.[2] At the beginning of September Commodore Moore was at the mouth of the Rio del Norte.

[1]Longitude.
[2]Diary of midshipman James L. Mabry, in *Galveston News*, January 16 and 23, and February 13, 1893.

September 19, 1840: . . . stood in chase of strange ship who hoisted Spanish colors, bearing two points on our lee bow. At 5:30 strange ship tacked and stood for us. Beat to quarters and spoke her. She proved the Spanish corvette Gueriro,[1] mounting 22 guns.

October 4, 1840: From 4 to 6, gales with passing clouds. At 5 made a vessel with a signal of distress, lying on the reef at the north end of the island (Labos[2]). Sent life boat on shore to inquire if any of the inhabitants could pilot a boat out to her. At 6 the boat returned, unable to obtain any information or assistance. . . . Sent life boat on shore to build a fire as a beacon to the vessel in distress. At 9, manned, provisioned and sent life boat and second cutter to the relief of the distressed vessel lying on the Banquilla reef. The second cutter returned, not being able to proceed against a heavy head sea. . . .

October, 6 1840: . . . at 3.30 the life-boat and second cutter returned, bringing the remainder of the crew, passengers and baggage.[3]

October 17, 1840: At 1,50 standing in for Tampico bar. . . .

October 18, 1840: . . . at 3.30 a sail hove in sight, standing for anchorage. At 4 she came to anchor a short distance ahead of us. She proved [to be] the English brig of war Racer. . . .

October 21, 1840: At 2 the second cutter was fired at 3 times from the shore and very narrowly escaped destruction, the balls striking very close to her. We directed a gun at the fort and fired it, but the distance was so great that it did not carry. . . .

October 23, 1840: At 2,30, Jas. Garrett, second gunner, died of the scurvy. . . .

October 21,[4] 1840: . . . S. O. Sawyer fell from the fore top gallant yard overboard and was lost. . . .

November 4, 1840: At 1 sent first cutter with 228 gallons of water, 1 bag of coffee, two bags of flour and ten boxes of vermicelli to the schooner San Jacinto, and the launch with two anchors and chain. The schooner was ashore, where she had been driven in a norther, having parted one of her anchors. At 6, sent the launch with the men to the San Jacinto. At 7, sent the first cutter to the San Jacinto with 217 gallons of water. The captain left the ship. At 7,30 the captain returned.[5] At 10, the first cutter returned. . . .

November 21. 1840: . . . at 3 the city of Tabasco hove

---

[1]Guerrero.

[2]Lobos.

[3]The wrecked vessel was the Mexican brig, *Segunda Fauna.*

[4]Either this entry is out of place in the original diary, or it was meant for October 24.

[5]See p. 33, below.

in sight. at 3.30 came to with larboard anchor. . . .
November 23, 1840: . . . at 11.30 General Anaya visited the ship. . . .
December 6 1840: The federal brig-of-war fired a salute of twenty-one guns. At 9,40 she . . . hoisted the Texian ensign at the fore and fired a salute of seventeen guns. At 10 we answered it.
December 11, 1840: . . . At 10 the Zavala came alongside of us and made fast to us.
December 13, 1840: At 6 called all hands to up anchor. Got under way and backed down the river with the Zavala. . . .
December 15, 1840: At 11,30 boarded and took in tow the Mexican schooner Florentine. . . . At 2,30 boarded the Mexican schooner Elizabeth and brought her to under our stern.
December 16, 1840: At 8.30 got under way and cast off the two schooners, giving them permission to proceed up the river. At 5.30 came to anchor off the town of Frenterrea.[1]
December 17, 1840: During the night, James Duffries, ordinary seaman, died of fever. . . .
December 22, 1840: at 3 p. m. Samuel Edgerton, commodore's steward, died of yellow fever. . . .
December 25, 1840: Sent for Dr. Clarke of the San Bernard to visit the sick.

In copying the log of the *Austin*, Midshipman Mabry had no occasion to describe the terrible experience of the *Zavala* in the storm of September 23. The following, from the Tennison Papers,[2] in brief language gives a vivid idea of the perils of the sailor:

23d September, . . . we went to Arcos where we expected to meet the Commodo[re] and obtain a supply of provisions from him—but unfortunately he was not there, and after waiting a week on half allowance we went to Laguna de Terminas to obtain provision. We got enough provisions there by giving draft on the Consul in New Orleans (fund being all gone) and we came here to get fuel enough to carry us to Galveston. We arrived off the bar of this river too late on the night of the 3d October to com in, and towards Morning we had a sever gale, and sea from North east, a little the worst many of us had even seen—how the old Zavala stood it bravely, and after losing our rudder, best anchor and cable, the main mast throwing the guns and about 400 eighteen pound shot, and all our grape and cannister overboard, cutting the salloon, ward room, steerage and berth deck for fuel, we

[1]Frontera.
[2]Tennison's Journals, folio 350, p. 1. For a more detailed description of the *Zavala* in the storm, see THE QUARTERLY, VI, 123.

came in here all well and hearty on the 7th October. The Hull of the Vessel and engines being not at all hurt.

The last notice of the *San Antonio* that has been found, respecting this cruise, is a line in the Tennison Papers: "The *San Antonio* arrived in port[1] Dec. 9, 1840, with the rems[2] of Mr. Treat, agent from Texas to Mexico."[3]

Relative to the doings of the fleet for the next few months the information is very meager, but a contemporary newspaper gives the following items:[4]

Last from the Fleet.

By the San Bernard, T. A. Taylor commanding, which came into Galveston a few days since, we are in possession of the last intelligence from the fleet. A private letter has been shown us, dated on board the Zavalla, San Juan Baptista River, Tobasco, Dec. 23d, from which we learn that this steam ship is in complete repair, and ready for service; that the whole fleet will not probably come in before March or April. Commodore Moore, on board the flag ship Austin, was in the harbor at Tobasco with the Zavala, but, in a few days, would proceed to sea, on another cruise.

The schooner San Jacinto went ashore in a heavy gale, a short time before the sailing of the San Bernard. At the time, she was anchored off the Arcas Islands, but having imprudently ventured to sea with but one anchor, she was driven by the gale high upon land, a perfect wreck. No lives were lost, and we believe her guns were saved.

It is rumored (on what authority we have not learned,) that the Federal authorities[5] in consideration of the services rendered by Com. Moore in reducing a small town on the coast, contributed $25,000 towards the expenses of the navy during the expedition.

Gen. Anaya is in command at Tobasco, and his forces are constantly augmented by the voluntary enlistment of the citizens. The most amicable relations exist between them and our naval forces.

Tennison states that, at the time of the departure of the *San Barnard* from Tobasco, it was the intention of the *Zavala*, with the *Austin* in tow, to proceed to Laguna for a sufficient supply of

[1] Galveston.
[2] Remains.
[3] Tennison's Journal, folio 352, p. 3.
[4] *Telegraph and Texas Register*, January 13, 1841.
[5] That is, Mexican Federal authorities.

fuel, and thence to Galveston. The *Austin,* leaving the *Zavala* after crossing the bar, was to proceed to the Arcos Islands, and thence to Galveston. Under date of February 10, 1841, Tennison further states that the *Austin,* on the cruise referred to above, boarded a small schooner, bound for Vera Cruz, having on board the Federal General Lemus, prisoner of the Centralists. By orders of Commodore Moore he was released, and was landed at Campeachy. Soon afterwards he was placed in a responsible position by the new government of Yucatán. On March 18, according to Tennison, the *San Bernard* returned to Galveston. She had touched at Vera Cruz, where her appearance was by no means welcome to the natives. Eight boats, with about seventy men each, had prepared to attack this single schooner manned by a crew of only twenty. The timely interference, however, of the British sloop *Comus* prevented trouble. On this trip the *San Bernard* had lost her foremast, and was forced to stop at the Arcos Islands for repairs. The *Zavala* was at Laguna on March 1, since her supplies of fuel and provisions had not arrived from New Orleans.[1] The following extract gives a glimpse of her at some later time:[2]

The steamship Zavala arrived yesterday in five days from Yucatan. She had on board $8460 in specie, having received ten thousand dollars in payment of services rendered by our Navy in the taking of Tobasco, the balance being expended in the payment of debts contracted there.

At Yucatan everything was quiet. No standing army to make subordinate the civil authorities to the military, as in many parts of Mexico. All kinds of religious worship was tolerated there.

Arista has joined Canales; but had no designs against Texas. He seems determined to overthrow the existing government.

We are assured by a passenger on board the Zavala that the Navy could, if permitted to make captures, not only defray its own expenses, but support the government.[3]

[1]Tennison's Journal, folio 354, p. 1; folio 372, pp. 1-2.

[2]*Austin City Gazette,* April 21, 1841, quoting from the *Galveston Morning Herald.* No copy of the latter paper is known to the writer, and no mention of it is made in bibliographies of Texas or Louisiana newspapers.

[3]The reader will recall Lamar's statement that the officers of the Texas navy were not expected to make captures while the Texas agent was in Mexico negotiating for the recognition of Texan independence, because Lamar considered that such a policy would be dishonorable. Mexico, in this instance, seems to have outwitted Texas in diplomacy. She kept the Texas agents in Mexico in suspense as to her final decision until her vessels arrived from abroad, no doubt having been informed by the Texas agents,

Under date of July 3, 1841, Tennison states that on that day the *San Bernard* arrived, presumably at Galveston, with Judge Webb on board. He says that Mexico had refused to treat with or to receive Webb as an agent to procure the acknowledgment of the independence of Texas.[1]

Of the Tabasco affair, Commodore Moore has the following to say:[2]

. . . went up the river Tabasco, captured that place . . . levied a contribution of $25,000 with which supplies were obtained from New Orleans to enable the squadron to keep at sea upwards of ten months . . . and there by kept the Mexican Navy from appearing off the coast of Texas to enforce the blockade. . . . We remained in quiet possession of the town of Tobasco for twenty-one days and had no shot fired at us as we were leaving. During this cruise one Mexican schooner was captured within five miles of Vera Cruz, sent to Galveston, condemned and sold for seven thousand dollars.

An item of interest in connection with the capture of Tabasco is given by Midshipman C. C. Cox in his reminiscences:[3]

But we had no fight. The enemy evacuated the town before we reached it—and after one night's stay we again dropped down the River—but a good many bags of silver were taken on Board our vessel at Tobasco and a portion at least of the same was distributed among the officers and men of the fleet as prize money. I think eight dollars was the share I got.

April, 1841, saw the return of the Texan vessels to Galveston, and the Yucatán expedition of 1840-1841 was closed. This expedition is in history frequently confounded with later expeditions to Yucatán.[4] Historians also allude to an alliance between Yucatan and Texas in 1840, but this alliance was not consummated in that, as a means of getting their proposals considered, Texas war vessels were under instructions not to molest Mexican commerce until their agency terminated.

[1]Tennison's Journal, folio 372, p. 3.

[2]Moore, *Reply to the Pamphlet by Commodores Buchanan, Dupont, and Magruder*, etc., 19.

[3]THE QUARTERLY, VI, 124. He is in error as regards "one night's stay." His illness at the time explains the error.

[4]Brown, II, 198; Thrall, *A Pictorial History of Texas*, 306. Thrall states "They were placed in the service of the revolutionary government of Yucatan," and "sailed 24th of June, 1840." See also *University of Texas Record*, V, 155, and Moore's *To the People of Texas*, 36.

fact until 1841. The taking of Tabasco was the result of an impromptu arrangement between Moore and the officials of Yucatán; the official alliance between Yucatán and Texas, concluded in 1841, was one entered into by the civil authorities of both countries, the conditions of which were specified in a document entrusted to commissioners. In this respect it differed from the arrangements of 1840, which were made verbal and consequently could be easily broken at the caprice of either party, or upon explicit directions to the commodore commanding the Texas fleet disapproving of his actions.

Soon after Commodore Moore's return to Texas he was again sent to sea for the purpose of surveying the coast of Texas. Increasing maritime interests rendered this survey very necessary. He briefly describes this labor in a publication directed to the United States naval officials:[1]

From May to November, 1841, the vessels were overhauled and the coast of Texas surveyed by Captain Moore, with the aid of schooners of the Texas Navy; a chart for the entire coast was made by him and published in New York by E. and G. W. Blunt, and in England by the admiralty. It is the only correct chart now in use by navigators . . . one of the officers whose name is attached to the published remonstrance to the honorable house of representatives has been in service on the gulf since it was published in 1842; he has doubtless had occasion to use it, and I can with confidence call on him to attest its accuracy.

The following item concerning the survey is from the *Telegraph and Texas Register*:[2]

The schooner of War, San Antonio, left Galveston on the 4th inst. for the Sabine Pass, having Com. E. W. Moore and several officers on board, for the purpose of commencing the survey of the coast. Col. G. W. Hockley, was a passenger on board. We are glad to find this important work commenced. The officers of our Navy can not at this season be employed to better advantage than in this survey.

They were actively engaged in the discharge of these labors until their recall in October by President Lamar on account of the

---

[1] Moore, *Reply to the Pamphlet by Commodores Buchanan, Dupont, and Magruder*, etc., 19.
[2] July 14, 1841.

alliance entered into between Yucatán and Texas, which we shall consider in the next chapter.

XII. ALLIANCE BETWEEN TEXAS AND YUCATAN.

The idea of forming an offensive and defensive alliance on the part of Texas and Yucatán against Mexico, was, no doubt, discussed between the Texas commanders and Yucatán officials, while the Texas navy was in Yucatán; and doubtless, on the return of the officers from their cruise, the sentiments expressed by these officials, were imparted to President Lamar. According to Senator Sam Houston,[1] the first overtures looking to an alliance were made by President Lamar. Houston says:

It was in the month of July of that year[2] that the Texas navy was subsidized to Yucatan, an integral part of the Republic of Mexico. The then President of Texas, Mr. Lamar, made a communication to the Governor of Yucatan, proposing to confederate with him to render aid, and to receive reciprocal aid from him. In conformity to the invitation originating with the President of Texas, a Minister arrived from the Government of Yucatan, then in a revolutionary state against Mexico, with proposals to obtain the navy of Texas, for the purpose of conducting a war against the central Government of Mexico. On the 17th of September, I think, the proposition was submitted by Mr. Badraza,[3] and accepted through the Secretary of State by the President of Texas. By the 18th the matter was consummated, and directions given to the navy of Texas immediately to sail, and co-operate in the defense of Yucatan against Mexico; or, in other words to aid and assist in the rebellion. This was done without any authority or sanction of the Congress or Senate of the Republic of Texas. It was a mere act of grace or will on the part of the President.

Col. Peraza arrived at Austin on September 11. On the 16th he addressed to Samuel A. Roberts, Secretary of State, a lengthy communication,[4] the main points of which were that Lamar had written the government of Yucatán that he was willing to co-

---

[1]*Cong. Globe*, 33d Cong., 1st Sess., Appendix, 1081; Moore, *To the People of Texas*, 27-29; Rejón, secretary of state of Yucatán, states that Lamar did make overtures July 20, 1841.
[2]1841.
[3]Col. Martin F. Peraza.
[4]Anonymous translation in Moore's *To the People of Texas*, 15-17.

operate against the common enemy; that Yucatán was threatened by an invasion from Mexico which its navy was not strong enough to resist; that the case was too urgent for Yucatán to wait for the assembling of its congress. Peraza then proceeds, "I will therefore merely say to the Honorable Secretary of State that I am fully authorized by my Government to contribute to the removal of any pecuniary obstacles which might perhaps for the moment embarrass that of Texas in putting her vessels in action"; and he goes on to say that Yucatán would pay for the purpose of getting the squadron of three war vessels to sea eight thousand dollars in advance and eight thousand dollars per month, so long as the government should deem it necessary for the squadron to remain in active service. Any prize made and any revenue of the Mexican government confiscated by Yucatán and Texas was to be divided equally between them after first paying the costs of the enterprise. On the next day Col. Peraza received a communication[1] from the Secretary of State of Texas, in which he says:

When therefore you tell us that you have reason to apprehend that the same despotism which for a time waged so savage and relentless a war against us, is preparing to attack the newly established liberties of your country, we can not hesitate to cooperate with you in preparing to repel the premeditated attack by sending such a portion of our Naval force to sea as may be deemed adequate to the service required of it.

That this Government may derive incidental advantages from sending its Navy to sea, . . . is not denied; but that these advantages will afford a just equivalent for the heavy expenses of keeping our Navy at sea, and for the shock such a ste[2] may give to our nation's credit abroad; and the loss we may thereby suffer; the undersigned apprehends, it is equally unnecessary for him to deny. The President therefore in accepting the pecuniary aid offered by Yucatan, on the terms proposed in your communication, towards the support of the Navy so long as it continues to cooperate with that of Yucatan, only discharges a duty towards this Government which a rigid and economical expenditure of the public money demands. . . . The undersigned has been instructed, taking your propositions as a basis, to state specifically the terms upon which the President will feel authorized to afford the Government of Yucatan the aid which she demands.

[1]Roberts to Peraza, in Moore's *To the People of Texas*, 17-19.
[2]Step.

The stipulations following are four in number, and the same as given in Peraza's letter except the second, which reads: "All captures made by Texan vessels shall be taken into Texas ports for adjudication, and all captures taken by Yucatan vessels shall be taken into Yucatan ports for the like purpose." On the same day, September 17, 1841, Col. Peraza accepted the Texas propositions. In a letter to the secretaary of state he says,[1] being conformable to the spirit of my instructions, they are sanctioned on my part in the name of my government, which is pledged to their most punctual and religious observance." In reply to this acceptance by Yucatán, the Secretary of State addressed a letter to Col. Peraza[2] in which he says in part:

the President has this day given orders, in conformity with the stipulations and agreements which have been mutually made between the two governments, for three or more vessels to proceed with as little delay as possible to the port of Sisal, when it is expected the Government of Yucatan will furnish the Commander of the Squadron with such information as will enable him to operate to the advantage of Yucatan. . . . It is hoped the action of Commodore Moore, who will personally command the squadron, will be such as to give entire satisfaction to the government of Yucatan. His orders have been made in strict conformity with the agreement which has been entered into between the two governments.[3]

On the same day, September 18, 1841, Commodore Moore received orders from the department of war and marine in conformity with the treaty entered into by Texas and Yucatán; and he was informed that the eight thousand dollars he would receive at New Orleans was all that he would be advanced for the provisioning of the vessels and recruiting of the men for the service. Another clause in the letter is here given in full, as Commodore Moore claimed that at a later time in his service to Texas he complied with the order it contained, and was for so doing outlawed, declared a pirate, and dishonored by the Texan executive, Sam Houston:

[1]Peraza to Roberts, in Moore's *To the People of Texas*, 19-20.
[2]Roberts to Pereza, September 18, 1841, in Moore's *To the People of Texas*, 20-21.
[3]Those desiring to go more fully into a study of the alliance may consult Rivera, *Historia de Jalapa*, III, 400-401, 514-515; Banqueiro, *Ensayo de Yucatán*, 42-45; *Niles' Register*, LXI, 66, 131, 196.

The Department can not conclude these orders, without reiterating that the eight thousand dollars placed in the hands of yourself, and such other advances as Col. Peraza, in behalf of the Government of Yucatan, may think proper to make you upon the contract existing between his and this government, are the only funds you can rely upon for fitting out and supporting the squadron under your command: and if these are insufficient to enable you to go to sea under these orders, you will not attempt it, but remain in port, without accepting or using any portion of the pecuniary contribution which the government of Yucatan has agreed to advance.[1]

On Friday, October 8, 1841, Lieutenant Lewis left Galveston[2] with the above dispatches and secret orders for Commodore Moore, to be opened after the completion of the provisioning. Commodore Moore was still surveying the coast, being on board the *San Antonio,* and accompanied by the *San Bernard,* commanded by Lieutenant Crisp. Lieutenant Lewis reached Moore on the 13th, and on receipt of the documents Moore sailed at once for Galveston. The money for the cruise and outfitting was deposited by the commissioner in the custom-house in Galveston. Within two months all preparations had been made; and, on December 13, 1841, the vessels under Commodore Moore sailed for Yucatán. Outside of Galveston Bar Commodore Moore opened his secret orders, and found that he was instructed to sail direct for Sisal, in the State of Yucatán,[3] and to co-operate with the sea and land forces of Yucatán in checking any hostile act of Mexico. He was also instructed to capture Mexican towns, and to levy contributions; and, for the purpose of compelling payment, he was authorized to destroy public works and edifices, and to seize public property, "taking care, however, to adhere to the principle that private property is always to be respected, and never to be violated except when unavoidable in the execution of duty." These acts it was hoped, would cause the central government no little annoyance, and would "strike a terror among the inhabitants, which may be very useful to us should it again be thought advisable to enter into negotiations for peace." For carrying out these instructions

---

[1]Archer to Moore September 18, 1841, in Moore's *To the People of Texas,* 12-13. Endorsed by Moore as having been received October 13, 1841.

[2]Tennison's Journal, folio 372, p. 4.

[3]Moore, *To the People of Texas,* 13-15.

of the secretary of the navy, the Texas navy has been criticised by historians. Yet the same methods were used in the Civil War twenty years later by both North and South.

The first official communication received from Commodore Moore was dated January 31, 1842, from the Texas sloop-of-war *Austin* at anchor off Sisal.[1] Accompanying his own letter are copies of letters exchanged between him and the officials of Yucatán, which illustrate the embarrassing situation in which he was placed on his arrival. They also show the estimation in which the Texas navy was held by the government of Yucatán, which was on the point of reuniting with Mexico, and was negotiating the terms with the commissioner, Quintana Roo, under the impression that Texas would not be able to comply with her engagements. But, encouraged by the arrival of the Texan fleet, it insisted on justice from Mexico; and the refusal led to a war, which for the time diverted the energies of Mexico from Texas to Yucatán.[2] Among other things the letter says:

Dec. 13, . . . I opened the "Secret Orders" received 1st October, in the presence of Lt. A. G. Gray, Purser N. Hurd, and Doct. Wm. Richardson. . . . I arrived and anchored off Sisal on the 6th inst,[3] the schooners San Antonio and San Bernard in company, having met the former on the 4th, and the latter on the 5th, . . . exchanged salutes with the Castle, and on the next day proceeded to the city of Merida, Lt. Com'g. Seeger in company with me.

The Yucatán political situation is next portrayed, and Moore then says:

The San Antonio takes this letter to Galveston and proceeds immediately to New Orleans for provisions, and when she joins me I will be enabled to keep at sea until the 1st May, without calling on the government for *one* dollar. If it be the wish of His Excellency the President to coerce Mexico to acknowledge our Independence, I can at once blockade all the ports of entry, viz.: Vera Cruz, Tampico, and the Brazos de Santiago; and if I had the steamer Zavala to co-operate with the Squadron, I could levy contributions on several of their towns to a greater amount than

---

[1]Moore to the Secretary of the Navy, in Moore's *To the People of Texas*, 21-36. The date of the letter as printed is 1841, which is clearly incorrect.
[2]Moore, *To the People of Texas*, 21.
[3]January, 1842.

the entire *cost* of the Navy—without the Zavala little else can be effected but to pick up any vessel that they hazard out. . . . The vessels building in New York when I left Galveston, for the Mexican Navy, I will use my utmost to intercept, and if they have contraband of War on board, I will send them to Galveston—this course being strictly in accordance with International law. . . . I leave to-day for Campeche and Vera Cruz; off the latter place I will cruize some time.

Commodore Moore was also instrumental in saving the cargo of the American schooner *Sylph* of New Orleans, which had been wrecked on the Alacranes, and he rescued the crew and sent them with the cargo to New Orleans in the *San Antonio*. He makes the assertion that the *Austin* was full of rotten wood and that the agent of Texas in supervising the construction of the vessels was grossly at fault. This reference was to J. G. Tod, and seems to be the beginning of the estrangement which in later years was emphasized by President Jones's nomination of Tod to take the place of Commodore Moore, who had been deprived of his position (illegally, Moore says) as commodore, by President Houston. While Commodore Moore was detained at Mérida, uncertain of his success in negotiating with the Yucatán officials, rumors of danger threatening him reached Lieutenant Alfred Gray, commanding the ship *Austin*. As Gray could not communicate with Moore, he considered it his duty to detain as hostages, until the commodore's safe return, the commissioners from the national government of Mexico and from Yucatán, who were taken from the American barque *Louisa* on their way to Vera Cruz.[1] Lieutenants A. Irvine Lewis and Cummings secured the commissioners and they were held until Moore was communicated with. As soon as possible he informed Gray that he was in no danger and directed him to release them. Moore said that under similar circumstances he would have done as Gray did; but suitable expressions of regret were addressed to the commissioners. In Commodore Moore's next report to the secretary of war and the navy, he makes mention of the capture of the Mexican schooner *Progreso*. By this vessel he sent to Galveston a letter in which he says:[2]

[1] Moore, *To the People of Texas*, 30-33; Tennison's Journal, folio 376, p. 1. These commissioners had been appointed to consider the reunion of Yucatán to the Mexican Federation.

[2] Moore to the Secretary of War and Navy, February 6, 1842, in Moore's *To the People of Texas*, 36.

I have this day taken as a prize the Mexican Schooner Progreso.
I was off Vera Cruz yesterday and *saw* one of the vessels built in New York for the Mexican Navy, and learn to-day that she has been in three or four days, and the other one is hourly expected.

A Lieutenant of Artillery (Mexican Army) was passenger in the schooner Progreso. . . . I intend keeping him, as I will all other officers of the government who fall into my hands, until I can hear something definite of the Santa Fé expedition.

The following is a contemporary account of the capture of the *Progreso:*[1]

Feby 22d 1842

Lut Wm. A Tennison of our Navy arrived on Saturday in charge of the Mexican Schooner Progresso captured by the sloop of war Austin in sight of Vera Cruz . . . on the 6th. She is ladened principally with Flour and Sugar. . . . When the Progresso left the schooner of war San Barnard was in chase of another Mexican vessel, which was stated to have on board a large amount of specie. . . . The San Barnard was to the windward of her and between her and the shore, and so certain was Com. Moore of the prize that we would not think it worth while to join in the chase. . . .

A general officer was captured on the Progresso when he saw the Texan flag run up he tore off his epaulettes thrust them in his pockets, but it was no use he was caught in the act. . . .

Sat-Anz[2] has purchased an old English steam ship carrying 4 guns of an English system, and if he has any spirit—with her and the New York Brig may offer Com. Moore a fight—nothing would be more welcomb to the Tars.

On February 25, when the *Austin* was again at anchor off Sisal, Commodore Moore learned from a pilot that the Mexican ship expected from New York was lost on the Florida reef on her way out, and the other Mexican vessels would not give him battle. The schooner *San Antonio* left Sisal on February 1, for Galveston with a letter from the governor of Yucatán to the president of Texas; and she was expected by Commodore Moore to meet him at the Arcas Islands on her return about March 1, 1842. From the Arcas Islands Moore intended to go to Laguna, at which place

---

[1]Tennison's Journal, folio 376, pp. 2-3; copied from the *Galveston Civilian*, February 22, 1842. See also *Telegraph and Texas Register*, February 23, 1842.

[2]Santa Anna.

he was to overhaul the rigging and paint the ships. On March 8, Commodore Moore writes from Campeachy:[1]

> I arrived here on the afternoon of the 6th inst., from the Arcas Islands, where I waited two days for the San Antonio without meeting her; on my arrival here her delay was accounted for by the sad intelligence of the mutiny on board of her at New-Orleans (to which place she went for provisions,) and of the murder of one of the most promising officers, Lieut. Fuller, whom I have ever known. I expect to meet Capt. Seeger at Laguna, for which place I leave to-night, and I will mete out to the rascals the *uttermost penalties* of the law.[2]

Moore sailed that night, and two days later he received the following official note,[3] recalling him to Texas:

DEPARTMENT OF WAR AND NAVY,
15th December, 1841.

Commodore *E. W. Moore,*
    Commanding Texas Navy.
    Sir.—I am directed by His Excellency the President to order that the squadron under your command return forthwith to the port of Galveston, and there await further orders. . . .
                                                Geo. W. Hockley.

In reference to this note Moore says:[4]

> No. 16 . . . was received outside Laguna Bar on the 10th March, per Schooner of War San Antonio, and was written, as will be seen by reference to the date *two* days after the inauguration of President Houston. It was the first communication that I had received since sailing, and although a peremptory order, I was compelled to disobey it. It will be seen by the subsequent letter from the Department (20) that the course adopted by me was approved by the President.

The letter referred to by Moore as approving of his disobedience to this order reads as follows:[5]

---

[1]Moore to Lemus, in Moore's *To the People of Texas,* 41-42.
[2]See also *Telegraph and Texas Register,* February 23, 1842.
[3]Hockley to Moore, December 15, 1841, in Moore's *To the People of Texas,* 43.
[4]*Ibid.*
[5]Hockley to Moore, April 14, 1842, in Moore's *To the People of Texas,* 50-51.

DEPARTMENT OF WAR AND NAVY,
April 14, 1842.

Com. E. W. Moore,
    Commanding Squadron.

Sir: Your dispatches by Capt. Crisp were handed into the Department yesterday. . . . Your proceedings personally, and of Courts Martials, specially, are approved, and the latter confirmed.

Concerning the order for the recall of the navy, Houston in his speech before the Senate of the United States, July 15, 1854, said:[1]

The new President[2] was inaugurated on the 12th of December following;[3] and we find by the records, that on the 15th of that month the navy was recalled forthwith, and ordered to the port of Galveston. The orders ought to have reached the navy in ten or twelve days. A pilot boat was dispatched to carry the orders to Commodore Moore, the commander; but that vessel, owing to peculiar influences at Galveston, or some other circumstances, was not permitted to reach Campeachy until the 10th of March following. On the first of May, I think it was, the fleet returned.
. . .

In this connection, it is necessary, in referring to Houston's order dated December 15, 1841, to correct a very gross error on the part of historians which has, so far as I am aware, never been challenged by critics. Yoakum,[4] in closing the chapter devoted to the year 1840, says:

The President's[5] health had been for some time very bad; and, getting no better, he obtained from the Congress a leave of absence, and about the middle of December retired from his official duties, leaving them to be discharged by the Vice-President.

That is all true, but in the succeeding pages Yoakum does not state plainly that Lamar afterwards resumed his duties as president, and the inference is left that his retirement was permanent, which was not the case. Thrall[6] makes a palpable error. He says:

[1]*Cong. Globe*, 33d Cong., 1st Sess., Appendix, 1081.
[2]Houston.
[3]1841.
[4]*A Comprehensive History of Texas*, I, 368.
[5]Lamar's.
[6]Thrall, *A Pictorial History of Texas*, 137.

The cares and responsibilities of office weighed heavily on President Lamar, and the severe strictures of political opponents affected his deeply sensitive nature, and he applied to Congress for permission to absent himself from the Republic. The request was granted, and during the last year the Government was administered by Vice-President Burnet.

The "last year" refers, of course, to 1841. It is, of course, too well known to require proof, that Lamar was the prime mover and cause of the Santa Fé Expedition of 1841, and that he furnished Col. McLeod with a proclamation to be given to the people of Santa Fé.[1] It is also well known that he was the promoter of the Yucatán alliance consummated in the months of July to September, 1841. Moore states in his pamphlet[2] that this alliance was originated and was carried out by Lamar in 1841. He did, on account of ill health, for a time retire from the presidential duties, but only for a time. His letter to Burnet implies also that it was only temporary; for it reads thus:[3] "Ill health has compelled me to ask of the Honorable Congress permission to retire from the discharge of official duty for the present." Bancroft falls into the same error; he says:[4] "The labors of office and the animadversions to which he was exposed, induced Lamar to apply to congress for permission to absent himself; and his request being granted, during the last year of his term, the government was administered by Vice-President Burnet"; and adds in a footnote:

From Dec. 15, 1840 to Feb. 3, 1841, the acts of congress were approved by David G. Burnet, after which date no signatures are attached to the acts passed in the copy of *The Laws of the Republic of Texas* in my possession, only the word "approved" with the date, being used.

This last statement, however, proves nothing, for in printing the laws passed during Houston's administration from 1841 to 1844 his signature never appears, though he did sign many of them. Those

---

[1] Eugene C. Barker, in *University of Texas Record*, V, 159; Bancroft, II, 333.
[2] Moore, *To the People of Texas*, 29.
[3] Hobby, *Life and Times of David G. Burnet*, 23.
[4] Bancroft, II, 343.

which he signed are, as the secretary of state explains,[1] simply marked "approved."

I have here devoted much space to proving that Lamar did act as president in 1841, because the historians so plainly infer that he did not, that the general reader and even the worker in Texas history is led astray. If their statements were accepted, of course Lamar had nothing to do with the Yucatán alliance of 1841; but, their statements being disproved, all doubt as to Lamar's having held the reins of government in 1841 are removed. The peaceful invasion of Texan territory by the Santa Fé expedition had its conception with Lamar, and became a calamity only because of circumstances over which he had no control. Had the mission been successful, he would have been heralded as the foremost statesman of Texas. The Yucatán alliance was timely and of great help to Texas, and has only been recorded with doubting language by historians because it was little understood by historians, and because of the bitter attacks made upon it by Houston in after years. Notwithstanding the great deference given to Houston's opinions, nearly all the historians give the Yucatán alliance and the conduct of the Texas squadron in Yucatán a left-handed compliment. Lamar never quit his station because he shrank from criticism, as historians have stated; on the contrary, in his own lifetime, an able biography of him appeared in a leading Texas publication,[2] and, according to it, he was willing that his reputation should stand or fall according to these two policies.

Commodore Moore remained at the port of Carmen, Laguna de Términos, from the tenth until the twenty-eighth of March, at which time, accompanied by the two schooners, *San Antonio* and *San Bernard*,[3] he sailed for Vera Cruz. He says:

... arrived off Vera Cruz on the 31st, and ran close in under the Island of Sacrificios to send in a boat to the United States Ship Warren. ... I discovered that the Steamer under the Castle was raising steam, and the Schooner now under Mexican colors was warping alongside of her. I immediately run up

[1]Gammel, *Laws of Texas*, II, 792.

[2]*Texas Almanac*, 1858, 109-114. The sketch was probably either prepared by Lamar or reviewed by him.

[3]Moore to Hockley, April 4, 1842, in Moore's *To the People of Texas*, 46-50.

the boat and began making preparations to give them a warm reception, (9 o'clock A. M.) standing out to get an offing, the wind being very light, and we being barely out of gun shot of the Castle. I remained near all day, passing once inside of one of the reefs forming the harbour, but they did not come out. The Warren sent a boat out to the ship, by the officer who came in her, I learned . . . that Mr. Thomas Lubbock[1] who escaped from Mexico, had sailed but a few days previous . . . for Laguna to join me; that night I sent the *San Antonio* back to Laguna for Mr. Lubbock, and stood to the N. and W. in Company with the *San Bernard;* the following forenoon I captured the Mexican Schooner Doloritas *nine* days from Matamoras bound to Vera Cruz, she was very near the land when we discovered her, and the super cargo and part of the crew made their escape in the boat . . . —she parted company yesterday for Galveston, and in the afternoon I landed the Captain Mate and boy with all their private effects at Point Delgada. . . .

I herewith enclose all the quarterly returns of this Ship and the *San Bernard,* a correct chart of the sea coast of Texas, a correct chart of the bar and harbour of Pass Caballo with the Labacca and Matagorda Bays, and a plan of the proposed break-water, by which *twenty feet water* can be made at the bar at a comparatively trifling expense, and there is after getting in, one of the finest harbors in the world. . . .

On the 3rd inst., within a few miles of Tuspan, we captured the Mexican Schr. "Dos Amigos," from Matamoros, bound to Tuspan, with a cargo of salt. I will dispatch her also to Galveston to-night or tomorrow, in company with the San Bernard, the Comd'r. of which vessel[2] will take this dispatch to the Seat of Government and return to Galveston with an answer and instructions for me, by the time I arrive there. I touch at Sisal to get *ten thousand dollars* which will be due on the 8th inst., when I will sail direct for Galveston, in pursuance of your orders of the 15th Dec. . . . there is every necessity of keeping the squadron at sea, and in a fighting condition, to prevent our Ports being blockaded and all communication cut off from the United States. Without the speedy return of our Navy on this coast, the navy of Yucatan will be captured or join that of Central Mexico, through fear, if nothing else.

In a letter of the next day,[3] he adds:

[1]A member of the Santa Fé expedition.
[2]D. H. Crisp.
[3]Moore to Hockley, April 5, 1842, in Moore's *To the People of Texas,* 50.

I feel it my imperative duty to urge upon the Department the necessity of fitting out the steamer Zavala, in order that we may keep the ascendency by sea and the communication open between Galveston and New Orleans.

Moore, in commenting upon his recommendation respecting the *Zavala* says:[1]

Nos. 18 and 19 . . . are letters from me to the Department; the latter[2] contains my recommendation to the government to fit out the *Zavala* which could *then* have been done at a small expense and saved from destruction, the most efficient vessel in the Navy; worth, $100,000, which has been lost to the country by the *wise economy* of government. . . . The wreck of the *Zavala,* now lying in Galveston harbor, is a melancholy evidence, of the *sort of economy* practised by President Houston!

In these remarks Moore is undoubtedly correct; for, by an act of the congress of Texas, approved by Houston,[3] the president of Texas was authorized to have the *Zavala* repaired, and at a later session another act was passed, also approved by Houston,[4] making an appropriation of $15,000 for the purpose. This authority Houston never used.

The following letter will explain the temporary discontinuance of the Yucatán-Texas alliance:[5]

His Excellency the Governor . . . has received notice that they[6] do not think of invading us at present, and that if they do invade at all it will not be for eight months or a year, for reason of the want of resources and the embarrassed position in which Gen. Santa Anna finds himself. The State can not continue paying all this time, eight thousand dollars monthly to the vessels under your command, as agreed with the Government of Texas, to which you are subject, and for that reason I inform you, without, however, considering the friendly relations being interrupted, which has been reciprocally preserved by both Governments; that, you can . . . retire with the squadron under your command, after the current month has expired. . . . The Governor does

[1] Moore, *To the People of Texas,* 45-46.
[2] Moore to Hockley, April 5, 1842.
[3] Gammel, *Laws of Texas,* II, 791.
[4] *Ibid.,* 813-814.
[5] Lemus to Moore, March 29, 1842, in Moore's *To the People of Texas,* 53-54.
[6] The Mexicans.

not doubt but that he can depend upon the assistance of Texas after the above indicated time has transpired.

Under date of April 22, 1842, Lemus adds:[1]

The want of funds has compelled the Treasury to give a bill for $4000 to complete the $12,208, which will be paid in thirty days after date, consequently Mr. Seeger has only received $8666.66 including the account of supplies, and an order for account of the Schooner San Bernard.

Commodore Moore now sailed for Galveston with the squadron; and arriving there May 1, 1842, and finding President Houston and the secretary of war and the navy, Col. Hockley, there, he personally handed the latter his final report of the cruise of the squadron, the most important parts of which are as follows:[2]

I parted company with the San Bernard on the morning of the 6th April, and in consequence of continued winds . . . did not arrive at Sisal until the morning of the 18th, when I met the San Antonio, she having on board Mr. Thos. Lubbock. . . . The same afternoon the brig of War Wharton arrived, and the next day I sent Lt. Comd'g. Wm. Seeger to Merida. . . . On the forenoon of the 23rd, the San Bernard arrived, when I received your communication of the 14th ult . . . And got underway—the brig Wharton, and schrs. San Antonio and San Bernard in company: the next afternoon we all anchored off Campeache. On the 25th, the Yucatan vessels of war, two brigs and two schrs.—went to sea, and as they passed us they lowered their flags *three times* which we of course returned. In the afternoon I received on board eight thousand dollars. . . . we all got under way at 1 o'clock A. M., (26th.) In the afternoon parted company with the Wharton off the Arcas Islands and pushed on for this place, where I arrived to-day, and anchored at 4 o'clock— the San Antonio in sight astern, but the San Bernard not, she will be up tomorrow.

XIII. THE MUTINY ON BOARD THE SAN ANTONIO.

On the evening of February 11, 1842, there occurred a mutiny on the Texan war vessel *San Antonio,* which had just arrived from Sisal and was lying in the Mississippi River opposite the city of New Orleans. When the principal officers had gone ashore, the

---

[1]Lemus to Moore, in Moore's *To the People of Texas,* 55.
[2]Moore to Hockley, May 1, 1842, in Moore's *To the People of Texas,* 60-61.

seamen in some way procured liquor and drank themselves into a state of intoxication. Their suspicious conduct was noted by the officers left on board, who began to prepare for an emergency, but did not suspect a mutiny. The sergeant of marines asked M. H. Dearborn, officer in charge of the deck, for permission to go ashore. Dearborn replied that no officer then on the vessel was authorized to give such permission and advised the sergeant to wait until the captain returned. The sergeant continued to argue the point; and Lieutenant Charles Fuller, who was for the time in charge of the vessel, came on deck and inquired the cause of the disturbance. Some of the men told him that they wished to go ashore. He then ordered the sergeant to arm the marine guard. This was done, and the sergeant probably gave arms to the crew also. He then approached Lieutenant Fuller and, after having first attempted to strike him with a tomahawk, shot and killed him. As Fuller's body lay on the deck, it was beaten with muskets and cutlasses; and two midshipmen were wounded in attempting to protect it. The mutineers then shut up the officers in the cabin, lowered the boats, and went ashore; but they were followed, and several of them were arrested, six at once, and others later.[1]

Soon afterwards the *San Antonio* sailed to join Moore's flagship, the *Austin,* on the coast of Mexico, carrying two of the mutineers and leaving nine in jail at New Orleans. On its arrival, Moore ordered the trial of these two by a court-martial, which convened on the *Austin,* March 14. One of them was sentenced to be hung, and the other was given further time to get evidence from New Orleans. These proceedings were approved by the Texan government.[2]

After Commodore Moore went to New Orleans to refit in May, 1842, he entered into a correspondence with Governor Roman of Louisiana concerning the prisoners remaining in jail there, and was informed that a requisition from President Houston would be needed to secure their surrender. The requisition was accordingly issued on September 12, 1842, and on September 15 Moore was directed to order a court-martial to try the accused as soon as the testimony of witnesses could be procured. The name of one of the

[1] See the *New Orleans Bee,* February 12; *The Picayune,* February 13; the *New Orleans Commercial Bulletin,* February 14; the *Telegraph and Texas Register,* February 22.

[2] Moore, *To the People of Texas,* 47, 48, 51.

mutineers was omitted in the first requisition, and a special requisition for him was issued on October 29.[1]

The prisoners lying in jail were surrendered to Moore just before he sailed for Galveston, April 15, 1843, and in accordance with the previous orders of President Houston a court-martial was ordered, which convened on board the ship *Austin* on April 16, at one o'clock. The court was composed of Commander J. T. K. Lothrop, president; Lieutenants A. G. Gray, J. P. Lansing, Cyrus Cummings, and T. C. Wilbur, with Surgeon T. P. Anderson as judge advocate. The prisoners were tried on the following charges: first, murder and attempt to murder; second, mutiny; third, desertion.

Of the prisoners, Seymour Oswald, sergeant of the marines, had escaped before the party was surrendered to Moore, and Benjamin Pompilly had died in prison, confessing on his death-bed that he had killed Lieutenant Fuller. The court proceeded to the trial of Frederick Shepherd, boatswain of the *San Antonio*. After the examination of several witnesses, Joseph D. Shepherd, one of the mutineers, turned State's evidence upon a promise of pardon by the president. But for this the prosecution might have failed, as the principal witnesses perished in the ill-fated *San Antonio*, which was lost in the Gulf early in September, 1842. The testimony of Shepherd developed the fact that the mutiny had been planned and agreed to by the crews of the *San Antonio* and *San Bernard*, while these vessels were off the eastern coast of Yucatán in January, 1842. It was proposed to sell the *San Antonio* to the Mexican government. Circumstances forced the postponement of the mutiny till the *San Antonio* reached New Orleans.

The verdict of the court-martial after a careful trial is recorded in the following document, which was signed by every member of the court:

TEXAS SLOOP-OF-WAR AUSTIN,
August 18, 1843.

COMMODORE E. W. MOORE:

Sir: We, the President and members of the court-martial, convened for the trial of Frederick Shepherd and others, have the honor to transmit to you the accompanying documents, being a true record of the evidence and minutes of the court.

[1]Moore, *To the People of Texas*, 93, 95, 99, 100, 105.

In discharge of the painful duty and the awful responsibilities imposed upon us, we have endeavored to confine ourselves strictly to the law governing courts-martial, and to the evidence that has been brought before us, and we have duly deliberated upon the verdicts returned.

In the trial of Frederick Shepherd, we are of opinion that there is no evidence before the court to prove that he was aware that a mutiny was to take place, or that he was in a situation to aid or assist in quelling one on the night of its occurrence. We have, therefore, found the prisoner *not guilty*, and recommend his discharge.

Of the prisoners Antonio Landois, James Hudgins, Isaac Allen, and William Simpson, we have only to say that we deem the evidence elicited at the trial of each and every one of them sufficiently clear and distinct to convict them each of the various charges and specifications preferred against them, and have therefore sentenced them to death.

We beg to call your attention to the evidence in the case of William Barrington, from which you will find that he was deeply engaged in the mutiny on board the *San Antonio;* but it appears in the evidence that he informed one of the officers that it was to take place. In consequence of this information, the court has sentenced him to receive one hundred lashes with the cats.

Of the evidence in the case of John Williams and Edward Keenan, we think it unnecessary to make any comments. Williams, you will find, is strongly recommended to mercy.

Very respectfully,

Lothrop,
Gray,
Lansing,
Cummings,
Wilbur.[1]

In carrying out the sentence of the court-martial, Moore proceeded with due formality. On April 22, William Barrington was punished with one hundred lashes on the back. On April 25, Moore had the sentence of each mutineer who had been given the death penalty, together with the laws governing the navy, read to him before the assembled officers and crew, and warned him to be ready to die the next day. On that day, when all were assembled and the necessary preparation had been made, he told the prisoners of his duty to see the verdict executed; and that, as it was

---

[1] *Cong. Globe*, 33d Cong., 1st Sess., 2160.

his first experience of the kind, he hoped it would also be the last. At noon the ship was hove to, and the four who had been condemned to death were hanged at the yard arm. Prayers were then read over each separately, and the bodies dropped into the sea.[1]

The conduct of Moore in executing the sentence of the court-martial which he had ordered was characterized, in a communication addressed to him by Secretary of War and Marine G. W. Hill, as murder; and, for this and other alleged offenses, he was, by order of President Houston, dishonorably discharged from the naval service of the Republic.[2] The action of the president, however, was sharply censured by a House committee of investigation of the Eighth Texas Congress; and, as to the charge of murder, a court-martial provided for by the same Congress declared Moore not guilty.[3]

XIV. MOORE'S EFFORTS TO FIT OUT THE FLEET AT NEW ORLEANS AND HIS AGREEMENT WITH YUCATÁN.

While Commodore Moore was awaiting orders at Galveston after his return from the Mexican coast, he received the following communication from the secretary of the navy regarding the *Progreso*:[4]

DEPARTMENT OF WAR AND MARINE,
Com. E. W. Moore,   Galveston, May 3rd 1842..
    Commanding Texas Navy.
SIR.—

His Excellency, the President, has instructed me, for reasons appearing to him upon the petition and showing of the party interested, to direct that the prize schr. "Progreso," lately captured and sold, be permitted to pass the blockade, at present maintained, on the part of this Government, against the ports of Mexico on the Gulf, and to *enter any one* of said ports without hindrance or molestation by the navy of this Republic. . . .

I have the honor to be,
        Very respectfully,
          Your most obedient servant,
Signed.   GEO. W. HOCKLEY,
                          Secretary of War and Marine.

[1]See *Cong. Globe*, 33d Cong., 1st Sess., 2160; THE QUARTERLY, VII, 223.
[2]Moore, *To the People of Texas*, 182-183.
[3]See p. 140 below.
[4]Moore, *To the People of Texas*, 61.

Moore says the *Progreso* took advantage of this passport, and sailed under Mexican colors from New Orleans with four hundred kegs of powder while he was there, and that he could easily have captured her but for his orders. About the same time, Moore received another order from the secretary of war and marine which follows:[1]

DEPARTMENT OF WAR AND MARINE,
Commodore E. W. Moore,   3rd May, 1842.
Commanding Texas Navy.

Sir,—You will proceed forthwith to the Port of New Orleans, United States, to refit—the Schooners San Bernard and San Antonio will proceed to Mobile for the purpose of receiving such supplies as will be furnished by our Consul at that place[2]—the officers necessary for the committal of the mutineers on board the San Antonio will proceed from Mobile to New Orleans for that purpose.

Convoy will be given to all transports of troops from Mobile or New Orleans to Corpus Christi. . . .

I have the honor to be,
        Your most ob't servant,
Signed.   GEO. W. HOCKLEY,
                         Secretary of War and Marine.

A third order to Moore bearing the same date as the two already given[3] directed him to enforce the blockade ordered by President Houston on March 26, 1842. The causes leading to the proclamation of this blockade of the Mexican ports are given in the introductory part of a pamphlet issued by President Houston as follows:[4]

My Countrymen:—Repeated aggressions upon our liberties—the late insult offered by a Mexican force advancing upon Bexar—and the perfidy and cruelty exercised towards the Santa Fe prisoners, all demand of us to assume a new attitude—to retaliate our injuries, and to secure our Independence.

The attempt to secure peaceable recognition of independence

---

[1]Moore, *To the People of Texas*, 62.
[2]Moore says that the consul at Mobile was unable to furnish any supplies.
[3]Moore, *To the People of Texas*, 63. The order is printed with the date May 3, 1843, but a note on page 201 corrects the date to 1842.
[4]*Address of the President to the People of Texas*, Apr. 4, 1842.

from Mexico was found to be futile. In a letter written to Barnard E. Bee on February 6, 1842,[1] Santa Anna said:

> I fully appreciate the problematic conditions of Texas; and I have before me the entire series of its consequences. I believe war to be necessary. I believe it a measure indispensable to the salvation of Mexico, and that her government will not faithfully perform her duties, if she does not strain her resources to the utmost, boldly to enforce a full confession of her justice.

Commodore Moore remained a week at Galveston, and pursuant to orders left on the 8th of May to fit out his vessels to enforce the blockade. He remained on board the ship *Austin,* and took with him the schooners *San Bernard* and *San Antonio.* To equip and provision the vessels and to pay the officers and men required a great deal of money, and Texan credit was low, but, while Moore had many promises of pay, he received very little cash. According to his own account he used of his private means and credit $34,700;[2] and in later years his claim was allowed by the Texan Congress.

About one month after reaching New Orleans Commodore Moore was almost ready to sail; but on June 6 Commander Lothrop joined the squadron with the *Wharton* and brought the following instructions from Secretary Hockley:[3]

> You will furnish Commander J. T. K. Lothrop with such men and provisions as you can procure for the brig Wharton, and proceed with the squadron under your command, with the *utmost possible despatch,* to enforce the blockade of the Mexican ports, in accordance with the Proclamation of His Excellency the President.

The *Wharton* had only nine seamen on board, was without provisions and ammunition, and would require an additional outlay of six thousand dollars to prepare her for the cruise. Though he had already strained his credit, Moore attempted properly to equip this vessel, meanwhile sending his brother to Texas for one-half of the appropriation of twenty thousand dollars made for the navy

---

[1]See *Austin City Gazette,* March 23, 1842.

[2]Moore, *To the People of Texas,* 67. In this pamphlet Moore publishes many letters to prove that Houston, while ostensibly advocating war and anxious for the navy to proceed to sea, withheld the money appropriated for the purpose.

[3]*Ibid.,* 71.

by the last Congress. In the letter which his brother bore Moore said:[1]

> . . . not *one dollar* of this amount do I contemplate throwing into circulation, but if I had it I would be able to raise a sufficient amount here on my own paper, using the Exchequer bills as collateral security.

So fully did Commodore Moore rely on receiving this small amount for such an important enterprise, that he shipped two-thirds of a crew for the *Wharton,* contracted for provisions, arranged the manner of payment, and had arrived at the certainty of being able to sail with the whole squadron in ten days after his brother's return, if his mission proved successful. We may imagine his disappointment when his brother returned, and he found that in place of the long-promised means, a shadow had been sent in the shape of President Houston's bond or obligation to pay over on Moore's requisition exchequer bills, when signed, to the amount of ten thousand dollars. The explanation sent along was as follows:[2]

> The President directs me to say . . . that he has pledged himself, in the papers, that no further issue shall be made of Exchequer bills until the meeting of Congress.

The bond was absolutely worthless to Moore, and meanwhile what he had procured for the squadron was fast being consumed, and his engagements for future supplies were forfeited. Two hundred and thirty seamen had been shipped for the four vessels; but at the announcement of the failure of the government to send any funds the officers were disheartened, the seamen commenced deserting, and there was every prospect of a complete failure of the expedition. In this extremity Moore left at once for Texas, and returned the worthless bond of President Houston. He arrived at Houston July 2, 1842, and was at once closeted with the secretary of the navy. Among other documents he placed the following in the hands of the secretary:[3]

[1] Moore, *To the People of Texas,* 72.
[2] *Ibid.,* 72, 73.
[3] *Ibid.,* 76.

The Navy of the Republic of Texas. 115

Mobile, 26th May, 1842.

SIR—Captain Seeger of the schooner of war San Antonio, visits Merida for the purpose of receiving the money for the draft of ($4000) four thousand dollars, given me last month.

I have also authorized Captain Seeger to make an arrangement with His Excellency the Governor, and yourself, for an additional amount of money to enable me to reach your coast at an early date, better prepared for a longer stay, and I sincerely hope that the Government of Yucatan can aid me.

I have the honor to be,
    Very respectfully,
        Your obedient servant,
Signed   E. W. MOORE,
                         Commanding Texas Navy.
To the Hon. PEDRO LEMUS,
    Secretary of War and Marine,
        Merida—Yucatan.

This letter clearly indicates that Moore was looking to Yucatán to renew the alliance and to help the Texan navy; and the secretary of war and marine and President Houston were well aware at this time, both from documents and from personal interviews, of his plans. Yet there is no word of disapproval or of protest. This should be remembered in connection with the subsequent condemnation of Moore for the adoption of such a policy without giving notice of his intention to the proper department.

On July 5, Moore addressed a communication to the secretary of the navy[1] in which among other matters he drew attention to the fact that for the past two years nearly every officer had served without receiving pay, that many seamen when their time expired had to be discharged without pay, and that not an officer in the navy had a commission. He also said that the *Zavala*, which was lying in Galveston harbor unfit for service, must be repaired at once and caulked and put in the docks at New Orleans; "if she remains where she is with the water in her, the worms will destroy her in six or eight weeks." Agreeably to his recommendation, these matters were at once brought to the attention of Congress and suitable relief was given by it. Appropriations were made for the support of the navy, for repairing the *Zavala*, and

[1]Moore, *To the People of Texas*, 78-79.

for carrying out other recommendations made by Moore;[1] but as Houston would do nothing, all proved unavailing. The *Zavala*, which he was to repair, he allowed to become a wreck.

Moore says[2] that he remained in Houston from the 2d to the 23rd of July trying vainly to get twenty thousand dollars that had been a short time before appropriated by the Texan Congress for the support of the navy. On the latter date he called on President Houston, who expressed his gratification at having just had the opportunity to sign another bill making an additional appropriation for naval purposes of $97,659. Houston then asked Moore when he would return to New Orleans, and Moore replied that it was useless to return "without the means of raising money to sustain the Navy." The president then refused to put the twenty thousand dollars Moore was asking at his disposal, but offered to give him a bond to be used in raising money on the faith of the appropriation. Moore said that money could not be procured in New Orleans by any such arrangement; that he had nearly exhausted his means and credit to sustain the navy and would go no further till he saw a disposition on the part of the authorities to aid him; and that he would return to New Orleans at once, "disband the Navy and leave the vessels to rot in a foreign port, as officers and men could not be kept on board without rations." The next day he wrote Houston a letter stating the necessity for his having the amount of the appropriation, and soon after he was furnished with exchequer bills to cover the whole of it except a small amount that had already been expended. But he found with the sealed orders which were given him, and which were not to be opened till he reached New Orleans, instructions to the effect that he was not to sell the bills outright, but only to hypothecate them, their value being thus seriously reduced.

The commodore arrived at New Orleans on July 31. He found the ship *Austin* leaking seventy-three inches a day, and at once made arrangements to put her in dry dock; other repairs were also needed on her and the *Wharton*. He now opened his sealed orders respecting the future action of the navy and found a proclamation of blockade for the Mexican ports, which was to be in force three

---

[1]Gammel, *Laws of Texas*, II, 813.
[2]*To the People of Texas*, 82-85.

The Navy of the Republic of Texas. 117

days after its publication by him in the New Orleans newspapers. One of the reasons given in the proclamation for its promulgation was that a former proclamation of blockade[1] had been suspended, with a view to refit the vessels necessary for its effectual enforcement.[2] It is likely, considering the time of Moore's arrival in New Orleans, that the proclamation was published early in August, 1842. On August 19, he writes to the secretary of the navy that "he has not yet succeeded in negotiating for funds to get to sea. The pressure in the money market is unprecedented, and Texas liabilities are almost worthless." On September 7, he reports having made some progress, but still lacks money; and asks that the *San Bernard,* then at Galveston under command of D. H. Crisp, be repaired so as to join the squadron. She was not repaired, but was blown ashore by a storm in the month of September.

On September 26, Moore received from Acting Secretary of War and Marine M. C. Hamilton a communication, dated September 15, containing the following statements and instructions:[3]

I enclose herewith, a copy of Proclamation, issued by His Excellency the President, revoking the order of blockade, published in March last, in reference to the ports on the coast of Mexico. Your "sealed orders" [for the renewal of the proclamation], dated 27th July, from this Department, are by consequence rescinded, and are hereby countermanded . . . You will not however, relax your exertions in consequence of it, nor will your activity on the Gulf be in the smallest degree impeded thereby. . . . You will proceed to sea without further orders; and . . . open your "sealed orders," which are herewith transmitted.

The proclamation revoking that of the 26th of March gives for its reasons that:[4] "treaties of recognition, amity and commerce have been concluded with Her Majesty's Government of England, in which stipulations are entered into embracing the recognition of Texian Independence by Mexico:" and "that mediation is now employed, as well as an offered mediation by the Government of the United States of the North." And it goes on to state that, these countries being desirous that the blockade should cease, Texas, be-

[1]That of March 26, 1842.
[2]Moore, *To the People of Texas,* 88-89.
[3]*Ibid.,* 95.
[4]*Ibid.,* 96.

ing under many obligations to them, therefore revokes the order of blockade; and only Mexican war vessels and vessels bound for Mexican ports laden with contraband of war will be liable to capture.

The sealed orders enclosed with the secretary's letter were opened by Moore on April 19, 1843, after leaving the bar of the Mississippi, and he found that they directed him to cruise up and down the Mexican coast capturing all Mexican vessels he might fall in with, "both armed and merchantmen," and capturing cities and laying contributions upon them. They contained the following general statement: "The Department having great confidence in your capacity and discretion as well as your knowledge of international law, deems it unnecessary to give more detailed or particular instructions."

A letter from Moore of October 14 reports, among other things, that on October 1 two midshipmen, F. R. Culp and George R. White, had fought a duel in which Culp was mortally wounded; and that on October 11 Captain Robert Oliver, commanding the marine corps, had died on board the sloop of war *Austin* of congestive fever. The same letter states that Moore has made every effort to raise funds, without success. On October 26 he again writes to the department that he cannot get to sea if the government does not furnish him with the means, that the terms of many of the seamen are expiring, and that unless they are paid it will be useless to endeavor to ship another crew. On November 5, Moore received a communication from the secretary of war and marine dated October 29, which said, among other things:

With respect to the detention of the squadron, I am instructed by His Excellency the President, to say, that he regrets it exceedingly—that it was very much to be wished that it could have been upon the Gulf; but that all the funds placed by Congress at the disposition of the Government for that branch of the public service, have already been placed at your command.[1]

Moore comments on this statement as follows: "Strange as it may appear, *not one dollar* of the $97,659 appropriated in July 1842, *had been or has ever been to this day placed at my command.*" In a communication from Hamilton to Moore, dated January 2,

[1]Moore, *To the People of Texas*, 100, 101, 104.

1843, this assertion is acknowledged. Moore says, "The evident intention of this paragraph in the letter, was to impress the belief on the minds of the members of Congress while in 'secret session,' (which was no doubt then resolved on by His Excellency) that I had received the whole of both appropriations. . . . Moreover, I have been informed by several members that such was their conviction."

Hamilton's letter of October 29 goes on to say:

Nothing has been received in reference to the schooner San Antonio since she sailed for the coast of Yucatan in August last. Has she since returned?

If you cannot with the means at your command, prepare the squadron for sea, you will immediately with all the vessels under your command sail for the port of Galveston.

This last clause contains the "order" to which President Houston in his proclamation of March 23, 1843,[1] refers as that for Moore's return to Galveston. This is the order that according to the proclamation was reiterated in the other orders that were disobeyed, and is the text for the various charges made against Moore of contumacy, disobedience of orders, mutiny, and piracy. If the reader examines the order critically, he can see that it was a provisional order for Moore to return to Galveston, if he found it impracticable to carry into execution the government's positive orders to prepare for operations against the enemy, which was still the desire of the government. Moore states that if this had been an unequivocal order for his return to Galveston, he would have been fully justified in postponing the execution of the order; for the enemy was daily expected upon the Texan coast, and the government of Texas would certainly not wish him to return to sea when unprepared to make such a defense as the vessels under his command ought to make.[2]

On November 19, 1842, Moore received from Acting Secretary Hamilton a letter, dated November 5, 1842, in which appears the following:[3]

Nothing can now be done with the San Bernard until appropriations are made for her repair. I much fear she is lost to the Gov-

[1] See *ibid.*, 168-170.
[2] Moore, *To the People of Texas*, 102, 103; THE QUARTERLY, IX, 22-24.
[3] *Ibid.*, 107.

ernment, and from accounts there is much reason to fear that the San Antonio is also lost, with those on board. If so, and it is impossible to fit out the two remaining vessels for efficient service, they had much better be in Galveston harbor than in a foreign port. With the hope, however, that some kind fortune may have enabled you to accomplish your purpose, I have the honor to be, etc.

The inference to be drawn from this, which is another of the "orders" cited in Houston's proclamation of March 23, 1843, is that if by any good fortune Moore can get his vessels to sea and cruise on the Mexican coast, he is to do so and the government will rejoice; but if not, then he is to come to Galveston.

The fears expressed regarding the *San Bernard* and *San Antonio* proved to be only too true. On September 22, 1842, Lieutenant D. H. Crisp writes Commodore Moore:[1]

The gale . . . drove me on shore and left me here in two and a half feet water. . . . I am getting everything out and putting on board the Galveston. . . . I am rather short-handed, having but 20 men, and four on the "list." . . . I think it will take me about two weeks from this to get afloat. . . .

October 24, Crisp writes Moore again, saying:[2]

I presume the best plan will be to repair her [the *San Bernard*] thoroughly and launch her— . . . at present I am doing nothing to her—my provisons will last about three days more, and then unless I hear something from the department I shall be obliged to discharge my men.

The navy appears to be *hard up,* and I think we are finished. . . .

I hope we may hear something from the "San Antonio" by the next arrival—I much fear that gale which drove me ashore capsized her—with my yards down it laid me on my beam ends, and I believe would have capsized me if she had not driven ashore. . . .

The boat has just arrived from Houston, and brought me no news from the department. . . . so I shall be obliged to discharge my men immediately, and when the officers have eaten up the rest, I presume they must discharge themselves.

[1]Moore, *To the People of Texas,* 108. Crisp's letter was written from the *San Bernard.*
[2]*Ibid.,* 110.

From the *Archer* Crisp wrote on November 2 that he had received a letter from the Department informing him that nothing could be done for him, and that he must do the best he could. On November 8, Moore sent Lieutenant Crisp from New Orleans such rations as he needed. These extracts from the letters of Crisp will serve well to show to what straits the naval officers were put to secure even the necessities of life.

The third of the "orders" cited by Houston in his proclamation against Moore was dated November 16, 1842, and was received December 1.[1] It simply instructs him to "carry out the instructions heretofore issued by the department, under date of 29th October and 5th November." Commodore Moore, on December 2, 1842, made reply to this letter, saying among other things:[2]

The San Antonio sailed from Galveston on the 27th August first for Matagorda and then for the coast of Yucatan—she having on board *over three months* provisions. . . . I did not mention her having sailed or the nature of her cruize, deferring it until her return, which I have been anxiously expecting for more than a month—but from news received from Campeche, two days since, up to the 15th November she had not been heard from, and I very much fear that she foundered or was capsized in one of the three heavy gales of September and October. The object of the cruize was to reconnoiter off the coast of Yucatan, and in the event of the people of that country holding out against the troops of Santa Anna, Lieu't Com'g Seeger was to communicate with the Governor and endeavor to obtain funds to fit out the Navy.

I received a letter from the Secretary of War and Marine of Yucatan in the early part of November, from the tenor of which I have been expecting funds from that quarter, but . . . I fear that nothing can be expected, . . . for the enemy are upon them by both sea and land. . . .

I have been compelled to discharge within the last month about *thirty men,* whose term of service have expired, and had not *one dollar* to pay them off; . . . and on the 14th inst. there are not more [than] *six* men in both vessels whose term of service will not have expired. Under this state of things the department will see the utter impossibility of moving the vessels from their present anchorage without means to ship seamen, . . . neither can towage or pilotage be obtained on the credit of the Government. . . .

[1]See Moore, *To the People of Texas,* 111.
[2]*Ibid.,* 112.

If I had money to ship a crew and purchase the balance of our provisions and clothing . . . I could sail in a few days, and as the enemy are now on the Gulf (blockading Campeche) . . . I would not hesitate attacking them with this ship and the brig Wharton—every officer in the service is anxious, exceedingly anxious, to get off.

In this letter Commodore Moore also sends to the auditor the returns of the pursers, N. Hurd and F. T. Wells, up to the quarter ending October 1, 1842. And again he speaks plainly of his desire to form an alliance with Yucatán, and indicates that Commander Seeger is there for that purpose as he has been at a previous time during Houston's administration. Afterwards Moore was denounced as a traitor for carrying out this plan; but the statement of his wish to do so evokes for the time no criticism whatever.

On the same day that Moore sent this letter to Texas, the acting secretary of war and marine sent a letter to Moore at New Orleans, which President Houston in his proclamation represents as the fourth order that was disobeyed. The letter merely states:[1] "Sir:—When you shall have arrived at Galveston and prepared your returns, as heretofore instructed, you will immediately proceed to this place, and report to the department in person." In reply to this fourth order, Moore writes December 19:[2]

I forward the muster rolls of the sloop "Austin" and the brig "Wharton" by which the department will see how many men we have to take care of the vessels. I am still making every exertion in my power to raise money to ship a crew and get out of the river; nothing from Yucatan since last I wrote—have definite information that the Mexican steamer "Montezuma" is on her way to Vera Cruz.

On January 12, 1843, Moore received from the navy department the fifth order named in the proclamation as having been disobeyed. It is dated January 2, 1843, and reads:[3]

Your communication of the 19th ult, enclosing muster rolls of ship Austin and brig Wharton has been received. Any expecta-

---

[1] Moore, *To the People of Texas*, 116; the letter was received December 14, 1842.
[2] Moore, *to the People of Texas*, 116-117.
[3] *Ibid.*, 117.

tions that may have been entertained of realizing or in any manner making available the appropriation of the extra session of Congress, will certainly end in disappointment. It was subject, from the first, and still is, to such contingencies as to render it a dead letter on the statute books. . . . You will, therefore, report in conformity (if practicable) with your previous orders, at Galveston.

It should be noted that the last order rests on the condition "if practicable," and that the letter transmitting it acknowledges receipt of the muster-rolls which Moore had sent to prove the impracticability of moving the vessels at that time. He had also become involved by the use of his credit to obtain supplies. It was apparently impossible, unless by the use of his already overstrained private resources, to move the vessels even to Galveston. The only hope that remained was that Yucatán, now closely besieged by Mexico, would advance the means for defeating the common enemy. Through two friends Commodore Moore received aid to dispatch a very fast pilot-boat, the schooner *Two Sons,* to Yucatán with a proposition to the governor of that state. It was dated on the sloop of war *Austin,* New Orleans, January 17, 1843, and the most essential part of it is as follows:[1]

His Excellency, the Governor of Yucatan. Sir—
. . . In the latter part of August last, I dispatched the schooner of war San Antonio to Yucatan with letters to His Excellency, Governor Mendez, containing certain propositions on my part, the tenor of which were, that if the government of Yucatan, would send to me the sum of $20,000 to fit the vessels under my command for sea, I would pledge myself to sail forthwith for your coast and protect it from the invading force of the Government of Santa Anna . . . The object in sending this communication to you now, in this manner, is to renew those propositions . . . if your Excellency will send to me by the schooner which conveys this, the sum of $8,000, I will, as soon after its reception as the utmost haste and dispatch will admit of, sail for your coast, [and] attack forthwith our common enemy, who are now blockading your ports. . . .
E. W. MOORE.

This proposition was favorably received by the governor of Yucatán, and Colonel Martin F. Peraza was sent to New Orleans with

[1]Moore, *To the People of Texas,* 119-121.

the money for which Moore had asked and with authority to conclude an agreement whereby Yucatán might obtain the services of the Texan fleet. The agreement was signed at New Orleans, February 11, 1843.[1] It was quite similar to the one that President Lamar had made with Pereza, as the agent of Yucatán, September 17, 1841.[2] The essence of it was that on condition of receiving from Yucatán money enough to get the Texan fleet to sea, Moore should sail as promptly as possible to Campêche and attack the Mexican squadron which was then blockading that port; and that after capturing this squadron he was to continue his coöperation with the Yucatecan government until the Mexican army should also be forced to surrender, for which service he was to receive eight thousand dollars per month. On February 24, Moore wrote to Acting Governor Barbachano of Yucatán[3] that he hoped to sail within a week.

The next day, however, arrived Colonel James Morgan and William Bryan, who had been appointed by President Houston commissioners to carry into effect a secret act for the sale of the Texan navy passed by the Texan Congress January 16.[4]

By the same steamer that brought them, Moore received a letter from Secretary of War and Marine Hill, which he opened in the presence of Colonel Morgan. It contained the sixth and last order cited in President Houston's proclamation of March 23 as having been disobeyed. On January 27 a letter was presented to Commodore Moore from the commissioners, enclosing another letter from the department of the same date as that previously received. The letter from the commissioners read:

New Orleans, Monday 27th February, 1843.
Sir:—You will receive herewith a letter from the Hon. Secretary of War and Marine of the Republic of Texas in regard to the vessels of the Republic under your command in this port: and we

[1] A translation is given in Moore, *To the People of Texas*, 125-126.
[2] *Ibid.*, 17.
[3] *Ibid.*, 129.
[4] There was a third commissioner, Samuel M. Williams, appointed, but he did not serve. The secret act has not been found; its provisions can only be inferred from the act of February 5, 1844, repealing it (Gammel, *Laws of Texas*, II, 1027), which refers to it as authorizing the sale of the navy.

should be glad to receive your report with as little delay as practicable.
We have the honor to be,
With every respect,
Your obedient servants,

J. Morgan,
Signed
To Commodore E. W. Moore,   Wm. Bryan.
Commanding Texas Navy.

The enclosed order read:

DEPARTMENT OF WAR AND MARINE,
Washington, 22nd January, 1843.

To Commander J. T. K. Lothrop,
Or officer in command of Navy,
Sir:—Immediately upon the reception of the order you will report the condition of the vessels, the number of officers and seamen under your command, to Wm. Bryan, Sam'l M. Williams and James Morgan, who have been commissioned by the President to carry into effect a *secret act of Congress with regard to the Navy,* and you will act under and be subject to the order of said commissioners, or any two of them, until you receive further orders from this department.

I have the honor to be,
Your obedient servant,
Signed   G. W. HILL,
[Endorsed:]   Secretary of War and Marine.
Received February 27.

Moore was recognized by the commissioners as the officer in command of the navy, and therefore as the proper recipient of the order they enclosed to him. But they had previously delivered him an order bearing the same date—January 22—from Secretary Hill directing him to leave the Texan vessels under command of the senior officer present and report without delay to the Department of War and Marine at Washington. Moore's explanation of his conduct in the premises is that he followed a well known military rule in obeying the order received last, there being no priority of date.[1]

Everything that passed between Moore and the commissioners was apparently harmonious; no serious misunderstanding seems to

---

[1]Moore, *To the People of Texas,* 130-132.

have arisen; they seem to have had entire confidence in Moore and to have acquiesced in his every suggestion; and there is no protest on record from either Morgan or Bryan. According to the orders Moore had received and obeyed, he was to be guided by what any two of them agreed upon. There was no friction, and they agreed on all matters. Then, was not everything done in a legal way? And if any one was to blame, was it not the commissioners rather than Moore? Their instructions read that "should sickness or any other cause prevent the commissioners from acting jointly, they or either of them, may act in all things separately and singly, but not adversely."[1] Another point in their written instructions was as follows: "Should Post Captain E. W. Moore, not forthwith render obedience to the orders of the department with which you are furnished, you will have published in one or more newspapers, in the city of New Orleans my proclamations."

On March 10, Moore wrote a letter to the secretary of war and marine[2] fully explaining his plans and purposes and his obligation to comply with his agreement with the Yucatán government. The arrangement, he said, was one greatly to the advantage of Texas, and could be ended any time that Texas so desired.

On April 3, 1843, Moore received from Acting Secretary of War and Marine Hamilton, in a letter dated March 21, 1843, the following order:[3]

In consequence of your repeated disobedience of orders, and failure to keep the Department advised of your operations and proceedings, and to settle your accounts at the Treasury, within three, or [at] most six months, from the receipt of the money which has been disbursed, as the laws require, and as you were recently ordered to do, you are hereby suspended from all command, and will report forthwith, in arrest, to the Department in person.

On receipt of this Commodore Moore at once wrote the following letter to the commissioners:[4]

[1]*Cong. Globe*, 33d Cong., 1st Sess., App., 1081.
[2]Moore, *To the People of Texas*, 137-138.
[3]Moore, *To the People of Texas*, 139-140.
[4]Moore, *ibid.*, 140. See also *Cong. Globe*, 33d Cong., 1st Sess., 2166; Moore, *Doings of the Texas Navy*, 11-13.

TEXAS SLOOP OF WAR AUSTIN,
New Orleans, April 4th, 1843.

Gentlemen—

The communication, dated 21st March, from the Department of War and Marine, was handed to me by one of you on the evening of the 3rd instant, and as there has been and is a singular erroneous opinion in the mind of the Executive in relation to my acts and motives, both of which are most seriously impugned, in order to preserve the Navy, (now ready for sea, with the exception of a few seamen) and save my own reputation, it is absolutely necessary that the tenor of the communication referred to above, should not be known to *anyone* until we arrive at Galveston, for which place I will sail direct, as soon as I get to sea; on my arrival, I will proceed in person to the Seat of Government agreeably to orders, and on my arrival at that place I feel assured that I can satisfy His Excellency the President, that so far from having any disposition to disobey orders, I have used every possible exertion to get the vessels in such a condition that I could venture on the Gulf. . . .

My "sealed orders" having been countermanded and others issued, I would be pleased if both, or either of you take passage to Galveston in the ship with me. . . .

I have the honor to be,
With high regard,
Your obedient servant,
E. W. MOORE,
Commanding Texas Navy.

Messrs. J. MORGAN and WM. BRYAN, New Orleans.

This letter gave entire satisfaction to the commissioners, and they united in the desire that Moore retain command of the vessels.[1] That the commissioners were entirely satisfied with Moore's action is shown by the fact that neither of them thought it necessary to publish Houston's proclamation; and they assured Moore that they were empowered by the president to act separately when it was not convenient for them to act jointly.[2] They made this statement to Moore, as he says, because he hesitated to act on the authority of one; and this he claims to have satisfied him.

[1] Moore, *To the People of Texas*, 139.
[2] *Ibid.*, 142.

XV. ENGAGEMENTS OF TEXAN AND MEXICAN NAVIES OFF THE YUCATÁN COAST AND HOUSTON'S PROCLAMATION AGAINST MOORE.

Commodore Moore left New Orleans with the ship *Austin* carrying eighteen guns and a complement of 146 men, and the *Wharton* with sixteen guns and 86 men, on the 15th of April, 1843. He was accompanied, in obedience to his invitation, by Commissioner James Morgan; and with him went also Colonel William G. Cooke, afterwards adjutant general of Texas. He arrived at the Balize on the 17th, and was there detained by the fog until the 19th. On the 18th the American schooner *Rosario* arrived and anchored near him, having had a passage of three and one-half days from Campeche. She brought intelligence of the capitulation of the Mexican troops under General Barragan, near the city of Mérida, and of the division of the Mexican squadron, the *Montezuma* being off Telchac. On leaving the mouth of the Mississippi, the direction of the cruise was changed, at the suggestion of Colonel Morgan, from Galveston to Yucatán. The reasons for this were given by Morgan himself in his testimony before the court-martial by which Moore was afterwards tried.[1] In answer to questions from Moore, he said that while the Texan vessels were still within the Mississippi River, there came on board the *Austin* the captains of two vessels who stated that they were just from Campêche; that the Mexican and Yucatecans were about to settle their difficulties; that Barragan and Lemus had capitulated; and that Ampudia was understood to be planning an expedition against Galveston. The witness had therefore hazarded the responsibility of suggesting to Moore to go by Yucatán, on the way to Galveston, to prevent if possible the formidable invasion of Texas that Houston had predicted. He expressed his conviction that Moore, without this suggestion, would have gone straight to Galveston. In a letter to Moore, dated June 3, 1843,[2] which harmonizes, so far at goes, with the evidence given before the court-martial, Morgan states that he wrote from the Balize near the mouth of the Mississippi to his colleague Bryan, who was still at New Orleans, not to go to Texas at once, nor to write to the Department of War and Marine till he heard further from Morgan

---

[1] Moore, *Doings of the Texas Navy*, 12-13.
[2] Moore, *To the People of Texas*, 171-172.

himself; for information obtained on the outward voyage might turn the squadron again towards Galveston. And Moore says that he and Morgan had received, just before leaving New Orleans, information that they regarded as credible to the effect that Mexico had pledged herself to England, in case she failed to prove her ability to reconquer Texas by taking Galveston before May 15, to agree to an armistice.[1]

Moore now sailed direct to Yucatán, and being much delayed by adverse winds, arrived at Telchac April 27, one day too late to meet the *Montezuma*. On the next afternoon he communicated with Sisal, where he learned that the *Montezuma* had passed but a short time before. On the evening of the 29th, he anchored within fifteen miles of Lerma, and the following morning at four o'clock got under way.[2] At daylight the *Austin,* under Moore's command, and the *Wharton,* under Captain Lothrop, discovered two large steamers, two armed brigs, and two armed schooners bearing down, evidently to attack them. The Texan vessels prepared for action and headed directly for the enemy. At 7:35 the Mexicans began firing. Some of the shot passed over the Texan vessels, and some fell short, but none reached their aim. At 7:50 the Texans began replying, and the engagement lasted till 8:26, when the Mexican vessels passed out of range of the Texan fire.

Moore then cast anchor within seven miles of Campêche. At 11:15 the two steamers again approached, and the fight was renewed between them on one side and the *Austin* and *Wharton,* assisted by two schooners and some gunboats belonging to Yucatán, on the other. At 11:40 the Texans, finding that their shot did not reach the Mexican vessels, again ceased firing. At 1 p. m. a few more shots were exchanged, but the distance made them ineffective. In the course of the engagement, the *Austin* was struck by one shot, which did no great damage. The *Wharton* had two men killed and four wounded. The Mexican vessels fared worse, losing fourteen men killed and thirty wounded. The *Guadalupe* had seven killed, and a number wounded.[3]

[1]Moore, *To the People of Texas,* 145-146.
[2]For the account of the engagement which followed, see Moore, *To the People of Texas,* 151-153.
[3]Midshipman Alfred Walke, Journal (MS. in Texas State Library) for April 30. Captain Cleveland, chief officer of the *Montezuma,* died

The relatively great loss in killed and wounded on the Mexican vessels is accounted for to no small extent by the fact that they carried much larger crews than the Texan vessels. They should have inflicted far more damage than they did; for the *Montezuma, Guadalupe* and *Eagle* carried in the aggregate four 68-pounders; six 42-pounders; two 32-pounders; and six 18-pounders, all Paixhan guns; besides, the Mexican fleet had the inestimable advantage of possessing two steamers. The vessels of the Yucatán squadron joined those of Texas during the fight, and in any estimate of relative strength must, of course, be counted with them. While the combined fleet carried two guns more than the Mexican, the broadside was very much lighter. Colonel Morgan testified[1] that the entire crew of the Texan vessels considered the affair a jubilee occasion, and the only regret was that they could not close with the Mexicans and fight it to a finish. He adds that both Commodore Moore and Captain Lothrop managed and fought their vessels handsomely. The wounded men of the *Wharton* were sent to the hospital at Campêche and were soon able to be about.

On Tuesday, May 2, Moore, after giving his crew one day's rest, endeavored to bring the enemy into action; but with their three steamers,—for they had now been re-enforced by the arrival of the *Regenerador*—they were able to keep directly to the windward of him and out of firing range. Moore maneuvered for three days without bringing the Mexicans to action; but on the afternoon of May 5 several ineffective shots were exchanged. On the 7th, a few minutes after sunrise, he undertook to close with the Mexican vessels; but they fled under steam and soon left the *Austin* and *Wharton* behind. Not a shot was fired during the day. In order to give his crew a little rest, Moore ran into Campêche on the afternoon of May 7 and anchored, waiting for a breeze to resume his maneuvers, while the Mexican ships anchored off Lerma, some six miles away. On the 10th he took advantage of the opportunity to

about the time of the engagement. According to Moore (*To the People of Texas*, 157), his death occurred on April 29 and was due to yellow fever; but Commissioner Morgan, in a report to Secretary Hill dated May 9, 1843, says it was understood that Cleveland was killed.

[1]Moore, *Doings of the Texas Navy*, 18.

The Navy of the Republic of Texas. 131

send a dispatch to Secretary Hill[1] acquainting him with the doings of the squadron.

Moore found on reaching Campêche that an armistice existed between Yucatán and Mexico, and that a treaty of amity was being negotiated under the impression that the Texan squadron would not come to the relief of Campêche. The naval battle of April 30 prevented the completion of the arrangement. While the vessels were at Campêche, the governor of Yucatán offered the loan of two long 18-pounders for the *Austin* and one long twelve for the *Wharton,* which Moore was glad to accept, and which proved very useful in the action that came a few days later. With the consent of the governor, these two guns were afterwards brought to Galveston.

On May 16, Moore succeeded in engaging the Mexican squadron again, and this time there was much sharper work.[2] The firing was begun by the Mexicans at 10:55, with the *Austin* about two and a half miles distant, the *Wharton* about one-fourth of a mile further, and the Yucatán squadron in shore near these two. At 11:05 the *Austin* replied with its long eighteen, and the *Wharton* began firing also. The engagement soon became warm and lasted until 3 p. m., when the *Guadalupe* ceased firing, and the Mexican vessels could no longer be brought to close quarters. In the course of the fight, the *Austin* was considerably damaged and lost three men killed and twenty-one wounded. The minutes of the action state that at one time Moore ran his ship directly between the *Montezuma* and the *Guadalupe* in seeking to close with them. The *Wharton* lost two men killed by the bursting of a gun, but was not struck by the Mexican shot at all. The Mexican vessels suffered greatly. The *Montezuma* was badly damaged, and the *Guadalupe* almost disabled; and the loss in killed and wounded on the two vessels, according to the testimony of an English deserter from one of them, amounted to 183.[3] In this fight, owing to the short range of its guns, the Yucatán squadron took no part. The Texan vessels threw a much heavier broadside than the Mexicans; but, inasmuch as the distance at which the greater part of the firing took

[1]Moore, *To the People of Texas,* 149.
[2]*Ibid.,* 160-162.
[3]Walke, MS. Journal, entry for May 16, 1843.

place made all except the long range guns unavailable, little can be inferred from the gross comparison. As Moore expressed it, the Paixhan 68-pounders of the Mexican vessels were tremendous guns, and the "hum" of their missiles was a "caution."

Among those killed in this engagement was Frederick Shepherd, who was one of the men charged with mutiny on board the *San Antonio,* but was acquitted. He was captain of a gun on board the *Austin,* and behaved himself with such gallantry as to win from Moore the strongest commendation.

On June 1, 1843, Colonel Morgan came on board the *Austin* from Campêche, bringing with him a proclamation by President Houston. This proclamation, though dated March 23, was not published until May 6, 1843. It is as follows:

PROCLAMATION.
BY THE PRESIDENT OF THE REPUBLIC OF TEXAS.[1]

Whereas, E. W. Moore, a Post Captain commanding the Navy of Texas, was, on the 29th day of October, 1842, by the acting Secretary of War and Marine, under the direction of the President, ordered to leave the port of New Orleans, in the United States, and sail with all the vessels under his command, to the port of Galveston, in Texas: and whereas, the said orders were reiterated on the 5th and 16th of November, 1842: and whereas, he, the said Post Captain, E. W. Moore, was ordered again, 2nd December, 1842, to "proceed immediately and report to the Department in person": and whereas, he was again, on the 2d January, 1843, ordered to act in conformity with the previous orders, and, if practicable, report at Galveston: and whereas, he was again on the 22d of the same month, peremptorily ordered to report in person to the Department, and to "leave the ship Austin and the brig Wharton under the command of the senior officer present:" and whereas, also, commissioners were appointed and duly commissioned, under a secret act of the Congress of the Republic, in relation to the future disposition of the Navy of Texas, who proceeded to New-Orleans in discharge of the duties assigned them and, whereas, the said Post Captain, E. W. Moore, has disobeyed, and continues to disobey, all orders of this government, and has refused, and continues to refuse, to deliver over said vessels to the said commissioners in accordance with law; but, on the contrary, declares a disregard of the orders of this government, and avows his intention to proceed

---

[1]Moore, *To the People of Texas,* 168-170; *Cong. Globe,* 33d Cong., 1st Sess., App., 1082.

to sea under the flag of Texas, and in a direct violation of said orders, and cruize upon the high seas with armed vessels, contrary to the laws of this Republic and of nations: and, whereas, the President of the Republic is determined to enforce the laws and exonerate the nation from the imputation and sanction of such infamous conduct; and with a view to exercise the offices of friendship and good neighborhood towards those nations whose recognition has been obtained; and for the purpose of according due respect to the safety of commerce and the maintenance of those most essential rules of subordination which have not heretofore been so flagrantly violated by the subaltern officers of any organized government, known to the present age, it has become necessary and proper to make public these various acts of disobedience, contumacy and mutiny, on the part of the said Post Captain, E. W. Moore; Therefore: I, Sam Houston, President, and Commander-in-Chief of the Army and Navy of the Republic of Texas, do, by these presents, declare and proclaim, that he, the aforesaid Post Captain, E. W. Moore, is suspended from all command in the Navy of the Republic, and that all orders "scaled" or otherwise, which were issued to the said Post Captain, E. W. Moore, previous to the 29th October, 1842, are hereby revoked and declared null and void, and he is hereby commanded to obey his subsequent orders, and report forthwith in person to the Head of the Department of War and Marine of this Government.

And I do further declare and proclaim, on failure of obedience to this command, or on his having gone to sea, contrary to orders, that this Government will no longer hold itself responsible for his acts upon the high seas; but in such case, requests all the governments in treaty, or on terms of amity with this government, and all naval officers on the high seas or in ports foreign to this country, to seize the said Post Captain, E. W. Moore, the ship Austin and the brig Wharton, with their crews, and bring them, or any of them, into the port of Galveston, that the vessels may be secured to the Republic, and the culprit or culprits arraigned and punished by the sentence of a legal tribunal.

The Naval Powers of Christendom will not permit such a flagrant and unexampled outrage, by a commander of public vessels of war, upon the right of his nation and upon his official oath and duty, to pass unrebuked; for such would be to destroy all civil rule and establish a precedent which would jeopardize the commerce on the ocean and render encouragement and sanction to piracy.

In testimony whereof, I have hereunto set my hand and caused the great seal of the Republic to be affixed.

Done at Washington, the 23 day of March, in the year of our

Lord, one thousand eight hundred and forty-three, and the Independence of the Republic the eighth.
Signed, SAM HOUSTON.
By the President.
JOHN HALL,
Acting Secretary of State.

On reading the proclamations both Morgan and Moore determined that it would be improper to attempt further hostilities against the enemy, and agreed to sail for Galveston immediately on receipt of sufficient powder to fight their way back if molested. The governor of Yucatán had none to spare; but he sent to New Orleans at once and procured what was necessary for the two vessels and for his own troops. This took several weeks. On the 25th of June the Mexican squadron left the Yucatán coast in the night, and the Texan fleet was in undisputed possession of the Gulf of Mexico. On the 28th of June the Texan vessels left Campêche and on the 30th arrived at Sisal. After remaining at Sisal a week and making such collections as were still due from Yucatán to Texas and paying all accounts made by himself and crew, Moore left the Yucatán coast with the thanks of the people of that country and their best wishes for his future welfare. After stopping at the Alacranes a few hours to catch turtles for his men, who were in need of fresh provisions, the vessels sailed for Galveston and arrived on the 14th of July, 1843.

Thus gloriously for Texas was the Yucatán expedition ended and the object of the cruise attained. The Texan navy rode in triumph upon the Gulf, and Galveston and Texas were free from apprehensions of an attack or invasion from Mexico by sea. That the outcome was so unfortunate for some of its worthy leaders, was no fault of theirs; and notwithstanding the shame brought upon them by Houston, the great majority of the people of Texas applauded and endorsed what they had done.

Notwithstanding Houston in his proclamation states, "that this Government will no longer hold itself responsible for [Moore's] acts upon the high seas," the government of Texas did nevertheless so hold itself responsible; and he, himself, be it said to his credit, afterwards approved two joint resolutions for the relief of certain disabled seamen, marines, and landsmen wounded in the action of the 16th of May off Yucatán.[1] Among the number awarded half pay for life were Dick Streatchout, Thomas Atkins, John Norris, Thomas Barnet, George Davis, James Brown, and Terence Hogan; while Andrew Jackson Bryant was to have the same pension, so long as his disability from wounds should continue.

XVI. DISMISSAL OF MOORE, LOTHROP, AND SNOW FROM SERVICE, AND TRIAL OF MOORE.

President Houston in his proclamation demanded of all nations in amity with Texas "to seize the said Post Captain, E. W. Moore, and bring . . . [him] . . . into the port of Galveston, that . . . the culprit or culprits [may be] arraigned and punished by the sentence of a legal tribunal." Yet, strange as it may seem, the president was averse to doing this, when the culprit presented himself; and it was only by Moore's own persistent efforts that he was able to get himself tried at all. On the day of his arrival at Galveston, July 14, he addressed a note to H. M. Smythe, sheriff of Galveston county, saying that, as he had been proclaimed by the president of Texas a pirate and an outlaw, he had voluntarily returned and now surrendered himself for the purpose of meeting the penalties of the law. The sheriff replied on July 15 that, as he had not been asked to take cognizance of the matter, either by the president or by any judicial authority, he did not conceive it incumbent upon him to do so.[2]

While Moore was yet on board ship, after reaching Galveston harbor, he received also a note from J. M. Allen, mayor, saying that the citizens and military of the city wished to give him a hearty welcome and begged that the hour of his landing might be fixed in accordance with their purpose. When he came ashore, he was received with the firing of cannon and the applause of crowds. He made a speech denying that he had disobeyed orders; and Colonel Morgan, who landed with him, also addressed the assembled throng, declaring that he assumed the responsibility for the cruise, and that under similar conditions he would do the same again.

On the 17th of July Moore reported his arrival to Secretary Hill;

[1]Gammel, *Laws of Texas*, II, 976-977, 1011.
[2]For both letters, see Moore, *Doings of the Texas Navy*, pp. 20-21.

and on the 21st of July he wrote again, saying, among other things.[1]

> I am . . . anxious to appear before the tribunal which his excellency, the President, has expressed so much solicitude to the world to have me brought before.[2]

On July 25, Moore received a letter, dishonorably discharging him from the Texas navy.[3] The charges recited in it are identical with those given in the proclamation of March 23; but in addition, he is charged with piracy, for having acted as commander of the vessels after being suspended, and with murder, for carrying out the sentence of the court-martial in the case of the mutineers of the *San Antonio*. On the same day William Bryan and William C. Brashear informed Moore by letter that Commissioner James Morgan had been discharged on April 3 and Brashear appointed in his stead; also that Commander J. T. K. Lothrop and Lieutenant C. B. Snow were discharged from the naval service of the Republic of Texas, and that Moore was authorized to turn over the command of the ship *Austin* to the senior lieutenant on board. Captain Lothrop was to turn the brig *Wharton* over to Lieutenant William A. Tennison.[4] The charges against Lothrop were disobedience, delinquency, and contempt of his superiors in refusing to assume command of the navy on the arrest of Moore, April 3, 1843, or to recognize and obey the order of the Department of War and Marine to the effect. Concerning this, Moore says:[5]

> As an evidence of the *extraordinary* course which the government has ventured to pursue, in order to crush her victims, I will relate the fact, that the President has *dishonorably* discharged a patriotic and meritorious officer, in consequence of *his failure to execute an order which he never saw*—and the authorities *knew* this fact when the discharge was penned!! The circumstances were these: A *sealed* letter was handed to Captain J. T. K. Lothrop in New Orleans, from the Commissioners, and was withdrawn by one of them (Col. J. Morgan) a few minutes afterwards, *before the Captain*

[1] For both letters, see Moore, *To the People of Texas*, 179-180.
[2] In this letter, Moore reports also the death of Lieutenant J. P. Lansing at Sisal on July 3.
[3] Moore, *To the People of Texas*, 182-183.
[4] *Ibid.*, 181.
[5] *Ibid.*, 10-11.

went on board of his vessel (where it is customary to open special communications.) It was returned, with the *seal unbroken,* when solicited by the Colonel who expressed himself pleased that it had not been read, as circumstances had arisen, which rendered its delivery no longer necessary. He gave no intimation of the character of the communication to Capt. Lothrop. All this was done by Col. Morgan with the full concurrence of the other commissioner (Mr. Wm. Bryan). It now[1] appears that the *sealed letter* contained an order appointing Capt. Lothrop to the command of the squadron in my place—and he has been *dishonorably discharged* from the service, for not thwarting the *Government Commissioners,* by ousting me from my command in compliance with a commission or order, which he has *not* seen to this day!!

Lieutenant Snow was dishonorably discharged for leaving the *San Bernard* in Galveston, when—as Moore claims—he was literally starved out by the policy of the government, and was going to join the squadron at New Orleans, carrying with him and depositing with Moore some small arms, which were liable to be stolen from the vessel he abandoned.

Moore and Lothrop, and apparently Snow also, acknowledged receipt of the communications dismissing them from the service. Moore had already, in his communication of July 21 to Hill, expressed his readiness and anxiety for trial; and, in his letter of July 28 acknowledging receipt of the notice of his dismissal, Lothrop, after protesting against his treatment, continued as follows:[2]

I claim and demand, a fair and impartial hearing for the charges brought against me, and as His Excellency and the Department have not thought proper to render me that common justice I shall at the proper time appeal to a higher tribunal.

Seeing that President Houston said nothing, in his annual message of December 12, 1843, concerning the dismissal of Moore, Lothrop, and Snow or the charges against them, Moore appealed to Congress. He gained his point; the naval committees of the House and Senate of the Eighth Congress made a joint report[3] that was

[1]September 21, 1843, the date of Moore's pamphlet.
[2]Moore, *To the People of Texas,* 179-180, 188-189.
[3]*House Journal,* 8th Tex. Cong., 348-361.

a complete vindication of Moore's character and conduct. Extracts from it follow:

In this case, Captain Moore was dismissed from a service in which he had made great sacrifices in sustaining the honor and reputation of his country, and deprived of a high and honorable station, which he had dignified by his official conduct and deportment, without a trial or even the semblance of a trial; and if such a course can be sustained or even excused in the functionary pursuing it, it must be under the provisions of some positive law. . . .

The undersigned know of no law that justified it. . . .

If, then, there is found no authority in the Constitution for the exercise of the power which was brought into action on this occasion, the committee are at a loss to know from whence it was derived. If there is any statute which confers it, the undersigned have been unable to discover it; but in their researches upon the subject, they have found a statute, which expressly declares, that it shall not hereafter "be lawful to deprive any officer in the military or naval service of this Republic, for any misconduct in office, of his commission, unless by the sentence of a court martial." This law . . . has never been repealed. It was therefore in full force and operation on the 19th of July, 1843, when Commodore Moore was dishonorably dismissed, and deprived of his commission . . ., "by the order of the President," without "sentence of a court martial."

So direct and palpable a violation of the positive provisions of a statute well known to the Executive at the time he gave the order, cannot be justified. . . .

The undersigned, however, cannot discover in the papers and documents submitted to them, the grievous offenses and crimes imputed to Captain Moore in the letter from the Secretary of War and Navy, conveying to him the order of the President for his dishonorable discharge. . . .

With regard to the first charge, the undersigned have found abundant evidence . . ., showing that he [Commodore Moore] had expended more money for the use of the navy, than he is charged with having received; they therefore consider this charge as wholly groundless. . . .

And thus the committee went through all the charges against Moore, finding them all practically groundless. On the seventh and last charge of "piracy" they comment in their report as follows:

Without investigating this new and singular species of piracy—a species which seems to have escaped the knowledge of most, if not all, the elementary writers on international law, the undersigned deem it only necessary to say, that the facts submitted to them do not sustain the charge. . . . Captain Moore was in command of the squadron by the authority of the commissioners, which command, conferred as it was by lawful authority, was a full and entire removal, for the time being, of the suspension and arrest, which was intended to be imposed by the order of the 21st of March, 1843. . . .

But whether Captain Moore was guilty of treason, murder, and piracy, or not, it forms no justification, in the opinion of the undersigned, for the violation of a positive statute in dishonorably dismissing him from the service without a trial, or an opportunity of defending a reputation acquired by severe toils, privations and hardships, in sustaining the honor and glory of the flag under which he had sailed and fought. If he were guilty, the courts of his country were open for his trial and punishment, and he should immediately upon his return have been turned over to those tribunals; and if not guilty, it was worse than cruel, thus to have branded with infamy and disgrace, a name heretofore bright and unsullied on the pages of our history; and to have driven from our shores, as an outcast upon the world, one whose long and well tried services, all appreciate and approve.

The undersigned, therefore, recommend the adoption of the accompanying resolution,

JOHN RUGELEY,
JAMES WEBB,
WM. L. HUNTER,
H. KENDRICK,
J. W. JOHNSON,
LEVI JONES.

The resolution recommended in the report, after reciting "that it is due to Post Captain E. W. Moore, to have a full, fair and impartial investigation of the charges," provides that, as a court-martial composed of naval officers cannot be convened, it is made the duty of the secretary of war and marine to convene, as soon as practicable, a court-martial composed of the major general of the militia, at least two brigadier generals, and other officers next highest in rank, who are to constitute a naval court-martial. It was passed by Congress, and Houston approved the resolution itself,[1] if not the finding. The court was composed of Major General Sidney Sherman, Brigadier General A. Somervell, Brigadier General E. Morehouse, Colonel James Reily, and Colonel Thomas Seypert; with Thomas Johnson as judge advocate. The trial commenced August 21, 1844, and closed December 7, 1844; and the decision was made public through the press January 11, 1845. The charges against Moore were willful neglect of duty, with six specifications; misapplication of money, embezzlement of public property, and fraud, with three specifications; disobedience to orders, with six specifications; contempt and defiance of the laws and authority of the country, with five specifications; treason, with one specification; and murder, with one specification. The court found him guilty under four specifications of the charge of disobedience, and not guilty of all the other charges. The report of the joint naval committee of the two houses of the Eighth Congress will show that the orders included in the four specifications of the third charge were in part conditional, and that the others Commodore Moore could not carry out and so reported upon the receipt of them.[2] Thus it will be seen that out of twenty-two specifications Moore was found not guilty of eighteen, and guilty, but in manner and form only, of four. Not guilty was the real verdict of the court and of the people, and it was so recorded by the only historian[3] that mentions the court-martial proceedings. Houston himself considered it a full and complete victory for Moore as evidenced by his vetoing the findings of the court with the statement, "The President disapproves the proceedings of the court in toto, as he is assured by undoubted evidence, of the guilt of the accused in the case of E. W. Moore, late Commander in the Navy."

XVII. FINAL DISPOSITION OF THE VESSELS OF THE NAVY.

When Moore and Lothrop returned on the 14th of July, 1843, to Galveston, with the *Austin* and the *Wharton,* the Texas navy had come to an end so far as active service is concerned. It

[1]Gammel, *Laws of Texas*, II, 1030.
[2]*Cong. Globe*, 33d Cong., 1st Sess., 2166; Moore, *Doings of the Texas Navy*, 23.
[3]Thrall, *Pictorial History of Texas*, 618: "The parties charged were honorably acquitted." By using the word "parties" Thrall probably means to include Lothrop and Snow; but these, of course, were not tried.

is true, however, that officers were still on the pay-roll, and if the occasion had come for the use of the vessels they could have been used with much effect. That the navy was intended to be used offensively if necessary, may be gathered from the provisions of an act approved February 5, 1844, authorizing the secretary of war and marine to contract for keeping the navy in ordinary.[1] The contract in the case of the ship *Austin,* the brigs *Wharton* and *Archer,* and the schooner *San Bernard* was to continue for one year unless those vessels should be required for the public service; and in that case the contractor was to be paid according to contract. It was further provided that the act approved 16th January, 1843, authorizing the sale of the navy, should be repealed.

Several writers have stated that the sale of the navy was never attempted; they probably gained this impression from the fact that the vessels remained in possession of the Republic. But the sale was attempted, as the following extract from an interesting and undoubtedly true account of it will show:[2]

All kinds of dire threats were made against any nation or individuals who should have the temerity to bid on the vessels. As the time drew near things waxed to the boiling point. Companies were organized and armed for battle to protect the country from the outrage to be perpetrated upon it. At last the day of sale arrived, the city was full of excited people, and Captain Howe was on hand with his battalion all in uniform and armed to the teeth. At about 11 A. M. an officer of the Republic appeared at the place of sale and announced the property for sale to the highest bidder. The people waited in breathless anxiety and with thumping hearts to see who was going to offer to buy. But after a short suspense it was knocked off to the Republic of Texas. You can imagine the effect of dropping a piece of ice on a white hot iron. The temperature went down like when a blue norther strikes the country. I venture to say; that the warlike spirit of Galveston has never been at so high a pitch, nor never been cooled off so suddenly since.

Lieutenant William A. Tennison was placed in charge of the vessels in ordinary and remained so until late in September, 1844, when, on account of sickness, he was relieved of the command, and

---

[1]Gammel, *Laws of Texas,* II, 1027.
[2]Emeline Brighton Russell, in *Galveston News,* October 20, 1901.

William C. Brashear was commissioned to take charge of them, Tennison being directed to report to him. Those who have followed the history of the annexation of Texas to the United States can easily understand why the navy was not needed after being placed in ordinary. It was because the United States government itself undertook the protection of Texas against Mexico from the day on which the treaty of annexation was signed, and because, just previous to that event it ordered a naval force to the Gulf for the purpose. The promise that such action would be taken was made by W. S. Murphy, the United States *chargé* in Texas, soon after the statute providing that the Texan fleet should be laid up in ordinary was passed.[1] The navy of Texas was therefore no longer a necessity; and it was left in ordinary until annexation took place.

The joint resolution by which annexation was effected provided that the Texan navy should be ceded to the United States. The transfer was made by Lieutenant William A. Tennison, who was then in command of the vessels, and he states that it took place in June, 1846. He was left in charge till August, when, finding that he was not recognized as an officer of the United States government, he turned the vessels over to the care of Midshipman C. J. Faysoux.[2] The vessels transferred were the ship *Austin* of twenty guns, the brig *Wharton* of eighteen guns, the brig *Archer,* eighteen guns, and the schooner *San Bernard,* seven guns.[3]

[1]Tyler, *Letters and Times of the Tylers,* II, 287-288.

[2]Tennison's Journal, folio 394, p. 1. There have been found at Washington only three papers relating to the transfer: 1 a list of officers of the Texan navy and a statement of pay due them; 2. an abstract of unpaid bills for supplies furnished the navy from February 16, to May 11, 1846; 3. a muster roll of the officers attached to the navy in ordinary, February 16, 1846.

[3]Thrall is in an error when he says, page 340, that the *San Jacinto* was one of the vessels transferred. The *San Jacinto* was lost in 1840 (see above, p. 90). He is also in error in stating that the *San Bernard* was destroyed in 1842 in a storm; she was only badly damaged and was later repaired. Finally, he is mistaken in saying that the *Zavala* was wrecked in the same storm. She was in bad repair early in 1842 and was run ashore on the flats in Galveston harbor to prevent her sinking. There she was permitted to lie until the worms made her unfit for repairs, when she was broken up and sold in 1844 (Moore, *Doings of the Texas Navy,* 6). Brown, II, 199, copies Thrall's errors.

XVIII. THE OFFICERS OF THE TEXAS NAVY.

When Commodore Moore and Captain Lothrop were discharged from the service by President Houston, the officers of the Texas navy, with but three exceptions, through sympathy with the discharged officers, and as an expression of their displeasure, tendered their resignations. No notice was taken of their action by the Department of War and Marine, and they were virtually in the situation of officers on leave of absence, without pay or the right to engage in any livelihood.[1] When annexation was consummated, they fully hoped to be attached to the United States naval establishment on the strength of the clause in the treaty of annexation providing that Texas, when admitted to the Union, should cede to the United States, among other means of defense, her navy. To the destruction of all their hopes, the Navy Department at Washington interpreted this to include only the vessels, and not the officers. Commodore Moore and others of the officers at once prepared a memorial and presented it to the House of Representatives, and it was referred to the committee on naval affairs. The committee, after carefully investigating their claims, reported a bill for their incorporation into the navy of the United States in comformity with the terms of the resolutions of annexation which formed the compact of union between the United States and Texas.[2] The method proposed was to repeal the limitation fixed by the statute of August 4, 1842, upon the number of officers and give the president authority to appoint the Texan officers to places in the service, with the proviso that these extra places should not be continued longer than they were held by the incumbents for whom they were specially provided.[3] The officers of the United States navy were bitterly opposed to this measure and appointed Commanders Buchanan, Dupont, and Magruder to direct their opposition. Their position was that the proposed arrangement would have the effect of elevating Moore, Tod, and others, who had been only lieutenants while they were in the United States navy, over those who

[1]Moore, *To the People of Texas*, 190, 191.
[2]*House Reports*, 31st Cong., 1st Sess., II (Serial No. 584), Rep., 288.
[3]Buchanan, Dupont, and Magruder, *In relation to the Claims of the Officers of the late Texas Navy*, 1.

were at that time their superiors; and of giving still others marked promotions without their having undergone due probation service. They interpreted the word "navy" in the resolution of annexation as meaning vessels only, and not including officers. This interpretation was in harmony with the opinion of the Supreme Court of the United States in the case of one of the Texan officers who had endeavored by *mandamus* to compel Secretary Mason to pay him his salary as an officer of the United States navy.[1] In this argument Buchanan, Dupont, and Magruder undoubtedly had the better of the Texans. But when they attempted to deal with the history of the Texas navy their statements are successfully challenged by Moore, and their arguments shown to be fallacious.

Special objections were raised to the appointment of either Moore or John G. Tod as an officer of the United States navy. A bitter fight was made against Moore on the ground that his dismissal from service by President Houston barred him from any participation in the benefits of the bill, even if it should be passed. In the midst of the controversy, a pamphlet containing, among other documents prejudicial to Moore, a copy of the message of President Jones vetoing a bill to return to him a portion of the money he had advanced for the use of the Texas navy on the ground that he was a defaulter, appeared in Washington. The publication and circulation of this pamphlet Moore attributed to Houston,[2] and in answer he wrote his *Doings of the Texas Navy*. In reply to the denial of his status as an officer of the Texas navy at the time of annexation, and to the charge of being a defaulter, Moore adduced the resolution of the Senate of Texas adopted June 28, 1845, declaring that his trial by court-martial was "final and conclusive";[3] and two resolutions by the House adopted the same day, one of which declared that the finding of the court fully entitled him to continue in his place as commander of the Texas navy, and the other that the thanks of the Republic were justly due him and those under his command in its service.[4]

As to Tod, the United States naval commanders thought he was

[1] Brashear *vs.* Mason, 6 Howard, 92, 99, 100.
[2] *Doings of the Texas Navy*, 3, 32.
[3] *Senate Journal*, 9th Tex. Cong., 2d Sess., 75.
[4] *House Journal*, 9th Tex. Cong., 2d Sess., 86.

The Navy of the Republic of Texas. 145

not justly entitled to be included in the list of officers connected with the Texas navy at the time of annexation, inasmuch as his commission as captain in the navy of Texas from June, 1840, was made out after the United States flag was flying over the Capitol building in Texas. Tod was given his rank by President Anson Jones, who was a bitter enemy of Commodore Moore. Jones interpreted Houston's act dismissing Moore as final and appointed Tod to take his place; and the United States officers claimed that, as Tod had never been confirmed by the Senate, his commission was a nullity. In order fairly to present Captain Tod's position, it is necessary briefly to recount some facts of his career.[1] It will be recalled that Moore had charged Tod with negligence when acting as agent, in allowing poor wood to be used in the construction of the *Austin*. Tod evidently sought redress at the hands of the Texas Congress, for shortly afterwards we find, upon the petition of Captain John G. Tod, a concurrent resolution introduced and passed thanking Tod for "his faithful and important services rendered to the country," and requesting the president to order a copy of the resolution to be read at the navy yard, on board each public vessel in commission, in the presence of officers and crew, and to be entered upon their log books. The president promptly sent a message vetoing the joint resolution of thanks to Tod; but the resolution was reconsidered January 31, 1842, and passed over his veto.[2] There is nothing to show whether or not 'Moore had to swallow this bitter pill. Captain Tod served Texas as a naval officer until 1842, when, at his own suggestion, in order to curtail the expenses of the government, he yielded his position. In later years when the Texan officers received back pay, Captain Tod was denied the benefits of the arrangement, the secretary of the navy insisting that his commission was void. Texans, however, would not admit the point, claiming that annexation was not fully consummated until the Republic of Texas yielded its power and authority to the State of Texas, which took place on February 19, 1846. Repeated resolutions of thanks and endorsements from the Texas Congress show in what high esteem Captain Tod was held in Texas; and at the request of the Texas senators and representatives Tod was at last

[1] See above, pp. 74-77, 99.
[2] *Senate Journal*, 6th Tex. Cong., 138, 139, 195, 198.

paid equally with the other officers connected with the Texas navy at the time of annexation.¹ He died in 1878.

The efforts made during the years 1847 to 1850 to get any favorable action from the government of the United States toward Texas naval officers ended in failure. In 1852 the endeavor was renewed; a joint resolution was passed by the Texas Legislature once more instructing the Senators and requesting the Representatives to use their influence to procure the incorporation of the officers into the navy of the United States reciting that "they are justly entitled to the same, as well from the construction of the terms . . . [of the treaty], as from their high characters, personal and professional, and the zeal, fidelity, patriotism, and valor with which they sustained the cause of this country during her struggle for Independence."² This effort came near being successful, but like the others it finally failed. It was not until 1857 that the few remaining Texan officers received any recognition from the government. The twelfth section of an act approved March 3, that year,³ reads as follows:

And be it further enacted, That the surviving officers of the navy of the Republic of Texas, who were duly commissioned as such at the time of annexation, shall be entitled to the pay of officers of the like grades, when waiting orders, in the Navy of the United States, for five years from the time of said annexation, and a sum sufficient to make the payment is hereby appropriated . . .; *Provided,* That the acceptance of the provisions of this act by any of the said officers shall be a full relinquishment and renunciation of all claim on his part, to any further compensation on this behalf from the United States Government, and to any position in the Navy of the United States.

The survivors benefited by this act⁴ were E. W. Moore, commodore; Alfred G. Gray, Cyrus Cummings, William A. Tennison,

¹Gammel, *Laws of Texas,* VI, 1063; *House Reports,* 46th Cong., 2d Sess., IV.

²Gammel, *Laws of Texas,* III, 1005; *Cong. Globe,* 33d Cong., 1st Sess., 2170.

³*Cong. Globe,* 34th Cong., 3d Sess., App. 427.

⁴The list of beneficiaries is taken from Tennison's Journal, folio 296, p. 4. I can find no list elsewhere. While this is not dated, it reads: "Officers who received pay from the U. S. Gov't," and could only apply to this act.

Charles B. Snow, and William Oliver, lieutenants; John F. Stephens and Norman Hurd, pursers; and the widow of Lieutenant A. J. Lewis. To this list must be added the name of Captain Tod, whose pay was turned over to his estate in 1883. Another claimant put in his appearance in 1858. This was Commander P. W. Humphries,[1] who was recognized by the Texas Legislature as entitled to the rank of commander in the navy of the Republic from July 3, 1839, to the date of annexation and entitled to pay the same as other officers. The midshipmen were barred by the secretary of the navy, and today the only survivor, so far as I know, George F. Fuller, of Ozone Park, New Jersey, is prosecuting his claim under the act of 1857.

It is a pleasure to note the kindly deed of the United States in thus assisting the former naval officers of Texas, who were almost without exception ill used by Texas, or rather by those in power in Texas. It must be acknowledged, however, that as a matter of right they had not the shadow of a claim against the United States. Even if the interpretation of the word "navy" in the resolution of annexation were construed to include the naval officers, the navy had been practically disbanded when Moore returned from Yucatán, and the officers sent in their resignations. That they should take advantage of annexation to put in a claim was natural; but the officers of the United States navy were right in opposing their admission, and Congress was generous when it allowed them five years' pay.

Below is a list of the officers of the second navy of Texas, which was furnished on application of Commodore E. W. Moore by Adjutant General C. L. Mann. Their appointments were confirmed by the Senate on July 20, 1842, and by order of George W. Hockley, secretary of war and marine, they were to take rank as their names appeared in the list. The dates of their commissions are given, and it is stated whether they were dead or alive on July 31, 1850. It will be noted that over half of them died within the short period of eight years.

Edwin Ward Moore, Post Captain, Commanding
....April 21, 1839, Alive

[1] Gammel, *Laws of Texas*, IV, 1152.

J. T. K. Lothrop, Commander..............July 10, 1839, Dead
D. H. Crisp, Lieutenant..................Nov. 10, 1839, Dead
Wm. C. Brashear, First Lieutenant..........Jan. 10, 1840, Dead
William Seeger, Second Lieutenant..........Jan. 10, 1840, Dead
Alfred G. Gray, Third Lieutenant............Jan. 10, 1840, Alive
A. J. Lewis, Fourth Lieutenant..............Jan. 10, 1840, Alive
J. P. Lansing, Fifth Lieutenant..............Jan. 10, 1840, Dead
George C. Bunner, Lieutenant...............Jan. 10, 1840, Dead
A. A. Waite, First Lieutenant..............Sept. 10, 1840, Dead
William A. Tennison, Second Lieutenant.....Sept. 10, 1840, Alive
William Oliver, Third Lieutenant...........Sept. 10, 1840, Alive
Cyrus Cummings, Fourth Lieutenant........Sept. 10, 1840, Alive
C. B. Snow, Lieutenant....................Mar. 10, 1842, Alive
D. C. Wilbur, Lieutenant...................June 1, 1842, Dead
M. H. Dearborn, Lieutenant.................July 1, 1842, Dead
R. M. Clark, Surgeon.....................Nov. 22, 1840, Dead
Thomas P. Anderson, Surgeon..............Sept. 10, 1841, Dead
J. B. Gardner, Surgeon...................July 20, 1842, Alive
Norman Hurd, Purser.....................Jan. 16, 1839, Alive
F. T. Wells, Purser......................June 10, 1839, Dead
J. F. Stephens, Purser...................Sept. 21, 1841, Alive
W. T. Brennan, Purser...................July 21, 1842, Dead

On Brennan's death, James W. Moore was appointed to take his place. In the list of those officers who petitioned Congress to be incorporated in the United States navy, appears the name of William E. Glenn,[1] "late master of the line of promotion." This carefully prepared list, added to the names mentioned in the body of the work, constitutes the *personnel* of the body of officers of the Texan navy.

A few additional notes regarding some of these may be of in-

[1]In Fuller's "Sketch of the Texas Navy" (THE QUARTERLY, VII, 223, 226), this name appears as "Wm. H. Glenn." Fuller also includes Robert Bradford and Edward Mason as midshipmen on board the *Austin* in 1842 and 1843 and Middleton on board the *Wharton*, and mentions that Dr. Peacock acted as assistant surgeon to Dr. Anderson of the *Austin*. He also states that in Walker's time, Faysoux commanded the whole Nicaraguan navy, consisting of one schooner with which he blew up the whole Costa Rican navy, consisting of one brig. Faysoux was afterwards mate of the *Creole* in its Cuban expedition, his commanding officer being Lewis, formerly third lieutenant of the *Wharton*.

terest. William Seeger was commander of the *San Antonio* when she was lost. A. J. Lewis died some time in the fifties. William A. Tennison was alive in 1858. Thomas P. Anderson, surgeon, had a son, Philip Anderson, who was living in Galveston in 1900. Mrs. R. W. Shaw of Galveston is a granddaughter of Norman Hurd. The midshipmen, being boys at the same time, have naturally been the last survivors. Of these Major John E. Barrow died in New York in 1902; W. J. D. Pierpont died in December, 1903. Of all the officers of the Texas navy, but one is alive today, Midshipman George F. Fuller, of Ozone Park, New Jersey. Commander Lothrop died in 1844 at Houston. Just before his death he took command of the steamship *Neptune,* running between New Orleans and Texas. But one name remains, and the tale is closed. Edwin Ward Moore finally procured from the Texas Legislature the passage of three acts providing that he should be paid for his services and reimbursed for his expenditures on the navy. It appears that by joint resolution approved by the governor January 24, 1848,[1] $11,398.36½ was allowed him. February 23, he was allowed a claim of three thousand five hundred dollars for commanding the navy.[2] Finally on February 2, 1856, was passed an act for his relief,[3] by which the treasurer was authorized to pay him $5,290.00, "Provided the said Moore shall first file with the treasurer a full and final release against the Republic and State of Texas for all demands." It has been asserted that he never received these moneys granted him by Texas. He at any rate received the compliment of having a county named for him in the state. Very little is known of him after 1837, but he made New York his home. He came to Galveston in 1860 and erected the old post-office building in that city. He took no part in the Civil War, and died in Virginia in 1865.

There is no question that Commodore Moore should be classed as one of the heroes of Texas; and this narrative may fitly be closed with the tribute paid him by the foremost officer of the Confederate navy:[4]

[1]Gammel, *Laws of Texas,* III, 334-335.
[2]*Ibid.*, 351.
[3]*Ibid.*, IV, 371.
[4]Semmes, *Service Afloat and Ashore During the Mexican War,* 49.

With an energy and ability possessed by but few men, he took hold of the discordant materials which Texas was collecting for the formation of a navy (a work, generally, of time and much patient toil), reduced them to system and order, and presented to the world the spectacle of a well-organized marine, bearing the flag of a Republic, not four years old!

Index

Abispa. Mexican vessel, 49, 50.
Admiralty, Court of, 57.
Adventure, Mexican ship, 54.
Allen, A. C., 8, 10, 45.
Allen, John M., Captain of *Terrible*, 26, 27, 135.
Anaya, General of Yucatan, 84, 85, 90.
Anderson, T. P., Dr., 83, 109, 148, 149.
Andrews, Edmund, 25.
Arcamble, C. S., Midshipman, 83.
Archer, Branch T., Dr., 7, 8, 47, 77.
Archer, Brig, 75, 84, 121, 142.
Asp, Texas vessel, 77.
Auld, Joseph, Ship's Carpenter, 83.
Austin, Henry, 45.
Austin, Stephen F., 2, 8, 77.
Austin, Flagship, 76, 83, 84, 98, 99, 100, 108, 116, 128, 129, 142.
Bache, R. Clerk, 83.
Baker, J. H., Lieutenant, 83.
Barker, Eugene C, 18, 82.
Barnett, Thomas, 23.
Barrett, D. C., 10, 11, 16, 33, 45.
Barrow, J. E., Midshipman, 83, 149.
Barton, Seth, 44, 45.
Bartlett, Dr., 48.
Baudin, Charles, Admiral French Fleet, 70.
Beatty, G., Engineer, 83.
Bee, Barnard E., Santa Anna's letter to, 113.
Bennett, L. E., 83.
Bernard, J. B. F., Midshipman, 83.
Betts, C., Midshipman, 83.
Bibliography. Authorities. See Preface.
Blockade of Matamoros, 58; of Mexican ports by French, 70; Mexico declares Texas ports blockaded, 82, 92; Mexican ports declared blockaded by Texas, 112, 116, 117.
Boston, U. S. ship, 26, 78.
Boylan, James D., Captain of *Brutus*, 49, 51, 54.
Bradburn, W. P., 55, 60.
Brashear, W. C., 83, 136, 142, 148.
Bravo, Mexican war vessel, 20, 25; Thomas Thompsan, Captain of, 63.
Brazos, 69, 77, Brig of war.
Brennan, William Thomas, 56, 60, 65, 148.
Brewster, W. H., 83.

Bronough, J. C., 83.
Brooks, Lieutenant of Marines, 42.
Brown, Jeremiah, Captain *Invincible*, 37, 42.
Brown, John W., Boatswain, 5, 81, 83.
Brown, William S., Captain *Liberty*, 39, 40, 41; Captain of *Invincible*, 57.
Brutus, Captures *Correo*, 9, 31, 32, 36, 38, 39, 46, 48, 55.
Bryan, William, 8, 38; Agent, 45; Commissioner, 124, 136.
Bunner, G. C., Lieutenant, 83, 148.
Burnet, David G., President, 30, 47, 52, 57, 108.
Burnley, Loan Commissioner, 67, 72.
Burns, Aaron, Lieutenant of Sloop *Opie*, 30.
Burton, Isaac Mayor, 47.
Bustamente, President of Mexico, 64.
Bynum, W. H., 8.
Calder, Roebrt J., Col., 30, 57.
Carleton, H., U. S. District Attorney, 6, 7, 38.
Carson, Samuel P., 36.
Cassin, Robert, Lieutenant, 60.
Cayuga, Steamboat, 37.
Champion, 32.
Charlestown, Steam Packet, 71, 74.
Chott, S., 72.
Christman, C. A., 83.
Clark, J., Captain, 84.
Clark, R. M., Dr., 83, 89, 148.
Clements, R. H., 83.
Cochran, Richard, Dr., 60.
Collingsworth, James, 58.
Colorado, Brig, 75.
Comanche, Mexican transport, 46.
Conrad, Edward, 45.
Consultation of Texas, 9.
Cook, William G., 29, 79, 128.
Cooke, Louis P., Sec'ty. Texas Navy, 87.
Correo, Mexicano, 1-9; captured, 54.
Correo, becomes Texan vessel, 37.
Cos, General, 2, 58.
Cox, C. C., Midshipman, 83, 92.
Crisp, D. H., Lieutenant, 83, 97; Captain, 102, 105, 117, 120, 148.
Crosby, Thomas, Lieutenant Marines, 56, 60.
Crout, James, Boatswain, 83.
Culp, F. R., Midshipman, killed in duel, 118.
Cummings, C., 83, 109, 146, 148.
Dallas, Commodore, 44, 52.
Damon, John, Lieutenant, 51.
Darocher, Captain, 60.

Index

Davis, Osky, Lieutenant, 51.
Davis, Mexican Captain, 63.
Dawson, Frederick, 72, 75.
Dearborne, M. H., 83, 108, 148.
Dearing, Lieutenant, 51.
De Kalb, Trading Schooner, 27.
Dinsmore, Silas, 16.
Dinsmore, T. S., Jr., 16.
Doloritas, Mexican schooner captured, 105.
Dolphin, 76, 84; becomes the *Wharton* later.
Dorey, Fletcher, Dr., 83.
Dos Amigos, captured, 105.
Dunn, Dr., 42.
Eagle, Mexican vessel, 130.
Eliza Russell, 49.
Ellis, Samuel, 45.
Errors of Historians: Edward, footnote 2; Pennybacker, footnote 2; Yoakum, footnote 6; Political Science Quarterly, footnote 18; Yoakum, 42; Texas Almanac, 42; Bancroft, 73; Brown, 75; Morphis, 75; Yoakum, 75; University of Texas Record, 82; Brown, 84; Thrall, 84; Brown, 92; University of Texas Record, 92; Yoakum, 102; Thrall, 102; Bancroft, 103; Brown and Thrall, footnote 142.
Estis, G. W., Lieutenant, 51, 60, 63, 83.
Everett, S. H., 36.
Falvel, Luke A., Captain of *Flash*, 29, 31.
Fannin, J. W., Jr., Col., 3; letter of, footnote 5; footnote 21, note 24.
Fanny Butler, Mexican transport, 46.
Faysoux, C. J., Midshipman, 142; footnote 148.
Finances of Navy, 20, 32, 38, 66-73, 79, 113, 116, 118, 123.
Fisher, S. Rhodes, 4, 20-24, 36, 45, 48-50, 64.
Flag, Navy of 1835, 16, 43.
Flash, the privateer, 29-31.
Flora, 32, 41.
Florentine, Mexican schooner captured, 89.
Foster, Robert, 42.
Franklin, Benjamin C., 57.
Franson, Fred, 42.
Fuller, Charles, Lieutenant, killed in mutiny, 108.
Fuller, George F., 78, 83, 101, 147, 149.
Galligher, Lieutenant, 51, 55, 56.
Galveston, Artillery Company, 29.
Galveston, Brig, 75.
Galveston threatened with invasion, 128.
Galveston honors Com. E. W. Moore, 135.
Gardiner, J. B., Dr., 83, 148.

Garlick, H. (S.), Midshipman, 83.
Gazley, 37.
General Council, 10.
Gibson, F. M., Capt., Marines, 42.
Gilmer, Commissioner of Loan, 42.
Goldborough, Hugh A., 83.
Gray, A. G., Lieut., 83, 98, 99, 109, 146, 148.
Grayson, Captain, Lieutenant of *San Felipe*, 5; Captain of *Oceon*, 31; Captain of *Yellowstone*, 32.
Grayson, Peter W., 58, 68.
Green, Thomas Jeff., 38, 45, 46.
Guadalupe, Mexican steamer, 129.
Gyles, Robert, 55, 60.
Hall, Edward, 5; footnote 20, 38, 45.
Hamilton, General, 71.
Hamilton, M. C., Acting Secretary War and Marine, 117, 116.
Hannah, Elizabeth, 20-24.
Harby, L. C., Captain *Brutus*, 51.
Hardeman, Bailey, Secretary of State, 30.
Harrington, E. B., 55, 60.
Harris, William P., 25; Captain *Cayuga*, 37.
Hartman, J. A., Midshipman, 83.
Hastings, Libel, Lieutenant, 51.
Hawkins, Charles E., Captain *Independence*, 37, 41, 55, 60.
Henderson, George, Lieutenant, 83.
Hill, Joseph, 56, 60.
Hill, W. G., 74, 111, 124.
Hinton, A. C., 69, 79, 80.
Hitchcock, L. M., Lieut., 51, 65, 68.
Hockley, G. W., Col., 93, 101, 107, 111, 113.
Holford, James, 71.
Hornsby, Henry, Lieut., 42.
Houston, A., 11.
Houston, Samuel, President, 17, 40, 41, 47, 49, 51, 54, 58, 65, 66, 74, 94, 99, 101, 104, 106, 112, 113, 116, 134.
Houston, 77.
Howard, G., gunner, 83.
Howes, Elijah, 43.
Hoyt, Captain of *Terrible*, 27; Lieutenant of *Brutus*.
Hubbell, H. A.
Humphreys, P. W., Lieut., 42, 147.
Hunt, Randall, Esq., 7, 9, 45.
Hunter, William L., 139.
Hurd, Norman, 51, 83, 98, 122, 147, 148.
Hurd, William A., Commands *San Felipe*, 4, 5; Commands the *William Robbins*, 20-22, 24; Captain *Brutus*, 37, 51, 56.
Independence, The, 32, 37-39, 53, 55-65.

Index 157

Invincible, The, 25, 32-39, 42-51.
Jacskon, O. P., 45.
Jackson, Thomas R., 36.
Johnson, F., Lieut., 42.
Johnson, J. W., 139.
Johnson, Thomas, Judge Advocate, 140.
Jones, Anson, President, 99.
Jones, Levi, 76, 139.
Julius Caesar, Captains Moore and Lightburn, 32.
Kelton, O. P., Dr., 42.
Kendrick, H., 139.
Kennedy, E. P., Lieut., 83.
Kerr, Peter, 21, 24.
Lacy, Lieut., 51.
Lamar, Mirabeau B., President, 70, 79, 82, 84, 93-104.
Lansing, J. P., Lieut., 109, 148.
Laura, steamboat, footnote 5.
Leay, C., 83.
Lee, Randolph, Lieut., 42.
Letters of Marque and Reprisal, 9-20, 65.
Leving, William H., Lieut., 42.
Leving, Purser, 55.
Levy, A. M., Dr., 51, 55, 60, 64.
Lewis, Ira R., 16, 20.
Lewis, Irvine A., Lieut., 83, 85, 97, 147-149.
Liberty, The, 25, 26, 32, 37-41.
Libertador, Mexican Brig, 51, 62.
Lightburn, Captain of Julius Caesar, 32.
Lipscomb, A. S., Secretary of State, 86.
Littlejohn, E. G., footnote 37.
Little, Pen, The, 49.
Lloyd, Daniel, 42, 83.
Logan, Lieut, 42.
Logan, W. G., 8.
Long, Secretary of U. S. Navy, 27.
Lopez, Commodore Mexican Navy, 63.
Lothrop, J. T. K., Captain, 56, 60, 83, 109, 113, 125, 130, 136, 148, 149.
Love, James, 76.
Lubbock, Thomas, 105, 107.
Mabry, James L., Midshipman, 87.
Marines, 36, 37, 51, 56, 83.
Marion, George, 55, 60.
Marstella, Captain of *Flash*, 29-31.
Matilda, Mexican sloop captured, 27.
Maury, W. T., Purser, 83.
McCormick, Michael, express rider, 30.
McFarlane, W. W., 83.

McKinney, Thomas F., 4, 5, 11, 16, 20, 25, 33, 38, 76.
McLeod, Col., 103.
Mellus, James, Lieut., 42, 55, 56.
Menard, M. B., 76.
Menard, P. J., 76.
Mendez, Governor of Yucatan, 85.
Merchant, Texas vessel, 77.
Mexican naval vessels, 129-131.
Minor, L. M., Midshipman, 83.
Montezuma, Mexican schooner, 11, 20, 33, 42.
Montezuma, Mexican steamer, 122, 128.
Moore, Captain of *Julius Caesar,* 32.
Moore, Alex., Lieut., 83, 84.
Moore, Edwin Ward, Commodore, 78-150.
Moore, James W., Purser, 83, 84, 148.
Morgan, James, footnote 37; Commissioner, 136.
Mutiny on *San Antonio,* 107-111.
Navy Affairs Committees, 12, 14.
Navy, Organization of First, 9-20; end of, 65.
Navy, Necessity of, 66.
Navy Yard at Galveston, 65, 69.
Navy, Reason why not active in 1840, 82.
Navy Vessels and Officers in June, 1840, 83.
Navy Fights and Captures:
  San Felips captures *Correo,* 5; *Bravo* and *Hannah Elizaabeth,* 20-22; *Thomas Toby* makes capture, 28; *Liberty* captures *Pelicano,* 40; capture of *Bravo,* 42; *Invincible* captures *Pocket,* 43; *Watchman, Fanny Butler* and *Comanche* captured, 47; *Eliza Russel* and *Abispa* captured, 49; *Invincible* fights two Mexican vessels, 51; *Brutus* captures rich prize, 53; *Union, Adventure* and *Telegraph,* Mexican schooners, captured by *Brutus* and *Invincible,* 54; *Correo* and *Raefaelita,* Mexican vessels, captured by *Brutus* and *Invincible,* 54; Mexican vessels destroyed, 55; *Independence* fights *Urrea* and *Bravo,* 56; *Independence* captured by Mexicans, 60-63; *Austin* captures *Florentine* and *Elizabeth,* 89; *Tobasco* captured by Texan Navy, 91, 92; Mexican schooner captured at Vera Cruz, 92; *Progresso* captured by *Austin,* 99-100; Mexican schooner *Doloritas* captured, 105; capture of Mexican schooner *Dos Amigos,* 105; *Austin* and *Wharton* engage Mexican Navy, off Yucatan April 30 and May 16, 1843, 129-132.
Navy, Second, measures to procure, 66.
Navy, act to lay in ordinary, 80.
Navy vessels disposed of, 140.
Navy officers, sketch of, 143-150.
Negroes, importation of to Texas, 3, 4.
Newcomb, Lieut., 42.

Index 159

O'Campo, Lieut., 6.
O'Conner, James, 40.
Oceon, steamboat, 31.
Oceon Queen, 31, 46.
Officers Texas Navy, sketch of, 83, 143-150.
Oliver, Robert, Purser, 83; Captain dies, 118.
Oliver, William, 83, 147, 148.
Opie, sloop, 30.
Parker, J. O., Midshipman, 83.
Parker, J. W. C., Captain, Marines, 83.
Pease, E. M., Secretary of Council, footnote 15.
Pelicano, Mexican trading schooner, 39.
Peraza, Martin F., Col., Yucatan Commissioner, 94-107, 123.
Perry, James, Lieut., 42.
Pierpont, W. J. D., Midshipman, 149.
Pocket, The, 43.
Postell, W. R., Lieut., 83, 86.
Potomac, The, 65, 68, 69, 75, 84.
Potter, Robert, 16, 29, 30, 36.
Power, James, 45.
Privateers, 13.
Progresso, Mexican schooner captured, 99-100, 111.
Pulaski, steamship, 68.
Raefaelita, Mexican, 54.
Randolph, Lieutenant of *Terrible*, 26.
Reiley, James, Col., 140.
Regeneradoe, Mexican, 130.
Richardson, William, Dr., 98.
Riley, Henry, 51.
Roberts, Samuel A., Secretary of State, 94.
Robertson, Arthur, Captain Marines, 37, 51.
Robertson, James G., 23.
Robinson, James W., Lieutenant Governor, 9, 35, 39.
Royall, R. R., 6, 22, 23.
Rugeley, John, 139.
Runaway scrape, 29.
Rusk, General T. J., 46.
Salter, John, 83.
San Antonio, schooner, 75, 79, 83, 84, 93, 97, 98, 104, 107, 119, 121.
San Bernard, schooner, 75, 83, 84-86, 90, 97-100, 104, 107, 117-120, 137, 142.
San Felipe, The, 1-9, 20.
San Jacinto, Battle, 30, 57.
San Jacinto, schooner, 75, 83, 84, 86, 90.
San Jacinto cannon, 64.
Santa Anna, Mexican President, 30, 31, 44, 46, 58, 70, 106.
Santa Fe Expedition, 103, 104.

Schofield, Hugh, 83.
Scott, J., 8.
Seeger, William, Lieut., 83, 98; Captain, 115, 148.
Sever, James, Lieut., 42.
Seypert, Thomas, Col., 140.
Shaughnessey, J. O., Lieut., 83.
Shepherd, William ., Secretary Navy, 67.
Sherman, Sidney, Major General, 140.
Smith, Benjamin F., 16.
Smith, Boatswain, 42.
Smith, Henry, Governor, 9, 11; footnote 21, 22, 23, 33-35, 60
Smith, L. H., Midshipman, 83.
Smith, William, Ship's Carpenter, 83.
Snow, C. B., 83, 136, 146, 148.
Somers, captures Mexicans, 22.
Somervell, A., Brigadier General, 140.
Stephens, J. F., 83, 147, 148.
Sterne, Adolphus, 8.
Stewart, C. B., Secretary to Executive, 15.
Stoneall, John P., Midshipman, 83.
Stuart, Ben C., 29, 31, 83.
Suares, Captain of *Thomas Toby*, 29.
Survey of Texas Coast by Com. Moore, 93.
Swartwont, Samuel, Hon., 47, 53.
Sweet, T. W., Lieut., 83.

Taylor, J. W,. Lieut., 56, 60; commands *Independence*, 61.
Taylor, T. A., Captain *San Bernard*, 90.
Telegraph, Mexican, 54.
Tennison, William A., Lieut., 27, 55, 60, 69, 83, 100, 136, 141, 146-149.
Tenorio, Captain, 1.
Terrible, Privateer, 26, 27, 59.
Texas, The, 77.
Thomas Toby, Priavteer, 27-29.
Thomas, Col., Secretary Treasury, 30.
Thompson, Alex., hydrographer, 65.
Thompson, Henry L., Captain *Invincible*, 42, 48, 50, 54.
Thompson, Thomas M., Captain, 2, 3, 6, 54, 63, 64.
Tobasco captured, 92.
Toby, Thomas, Texas Agent, 29.
Tod, John G., Captain, 74-77, 99, 143-146.
Travis, William B., 1.
Treat, Commissioner of Texas to Mexico, 38, 86, 90, 91.
Trinity, sloop, 75.
Tucker, J. J., 83.
Twin Sisters, the San Jacinto Cannon, 30.

Ugartechea, Colonel, 2.
Underhill, C. B., 83.

Index 161

Union, schooner, 31; Mexican schooner, 54.
Urrea, Mexican, 56.
Vencedor del Alamo, Mexican Brig of War, 31, 46, 51, 62.
Vera Cruzana, Mexican war vessel, 11.
Waite, Alfred A., 42, 148.
Walke, Alfred, Midshipman, footnote 129.
Walker, A., Midshipman, 83. No doubt same as A. Walke.
Waller, 37.
Ward, F., Lieut., Marines, 42.
Warren, U. S. sloop, 44.
Watchman, Mexican transport, 46.
Webb, Judge, Commissioner to Mexico, 92, 139.
Wells, E. F. (T.), 42, 83; Purser, 122, 148.
Westren, T. G., 45.
Wezman, E. A., 83.
Wharton, John A., 17, 65, 68, 77.
Wharton, The, brig, 76, 83; formerly *Dolphin*, 84, 86, 107, 113, 128, 142.
Wheeler, James H., Midshipman, 83.
Wheelright, George W., Captain, 37, 39, 54, 56, 60, 62, 64, 83.
White, George R., Midshipman, 118.
Whiting, Samuel, Major, 15, 16.
Whitmore, Midshipman, 60.
Whitney, 72.
Wilbur (D.), T. C., Lieut., 109, 148.
William Robbins, privateer, 5, 16, 20-26.
Williams, Samuel M., 4, 11, 45, 68, 71-73; note 124.
Williamson, William S., Lieut., 69, 83.
Wilson, R., 45.
Wood, Thomas, Jr., Lieut., 83.
Wright, Frank B., Lieut., 56.
Yates, A. J., 8.
Yellow Stone, 32, 58.
Yucatan Alliance, 92-107.
Yucatan Expedition, 1840-41, 92.
Yucatan Official Alliance, 93, 94-107, 123.
Yucatan Naval Force, 85.
Yucatan, revolt of, 81, 84, 85, 98.
Zavala, Lorenzo de, 30, 37.
Zavala, The, 72, 75, 77, 79, 80, 83-87, 89-91, 106, 115.

www.ingramcontent.com/pod-product-compliance
Lightning Source LLC
Chambersburg PA
CBHW071204160426
43196CB00011B/2191